Being Well

CHALLENGES *in* ETHICS

Being Well

Kenneth L. Vaux

Abingdon Press, Nashville

BEING WELL

Copyright © 1997 by Abingdon Press

Library of Congress Cataloging-in-Publication Data

Vaux, Kenneth L., 1939–
    Being well/Kenneth L. Vaux.
        p.   cm.—(Challenges in ethics series)
    Includes bibliographical references.
    ISBN 0-687-10943-4 (pbk. : alk. paper)
        1. Health—Religious aspects—Christianity. 2. Christian ethics.
    3. Technology—Religious aspects—Christianity. I. Title.
    II. Series.
    BT732.V38   1997   97-6714
    261.5'6—dc21

97 98 99 00 01 02 03 04 05 06 — 10 9 8 7 6 5 4 3 2 1

MANUFACTURED IN THE UNITED STATES OF AMERICA

— CONTENTS —

– Preface –

This book is the result of three decades of involvement in the scientific and technological institutions that so profoundly shape modern life. It represents an attempt to build a fundamental religious and philosophical structure on which to ground sound ethical theory and specific moral decisions on concrete problems of personal and public choice. While the principal concerns of my work have been in the life sciences and medicine, an attempt has been made to bring the broad insights of history, science, and theology to bear on practical problems in various endeavors, including health care, economics, and education. Anyone who works in this field knows the frustration of relating the demanding parade of immediate problems to a normative framework.

I have enjoyed the immense benefit of serving in three academic centers that emphasize the connection between spiritual and ethical matters and the scientific. The Institute of Religion in the Texas Medical Center in Houston, the University of Illinois Medical Center in Chicago, and Garrett-Evangelical Theological Seminary at Northwestern University in Evanston—all are great centers of interdisciplinary learning, where the ethical challenges of our civilization are the subject of rigorous activistic analysis. The colleagues and students in these centers have indulged this dilettantism and panoramic mind, allowing it to venture encyclopedically and resist the demand of modern academe for hyperspecificity. I thank especially Doug and Valerie James and Sara Vaux for their good counsel and assistance. To these partners in the quest, I dedicate this book.

Kenneth Vaux
Evanston, Illinois
New Year, 1997

– INTRODUCTION –

B eneath the placid surface of the smooth rational and technological life today, one feels the turbulence of new ascetic,
mystic, visionary, and humanistic impulses. On the one
hand, we experience an anxiety and dread about what we are doing
to ourselves and our world. On the other hand, at the level of
nations, we express a frugality that seeks meaning in the presence
of our affluence. At the same time, nations rush forward in compe-
tition and development. Kahn and Wiener began their assessment
of our technological age by noting that the quest for meaning is
surging to the forefront of consciousness.[1] In our relationship to
the environment we invoke a new harmony that listens more
responsibly to nature, all the while despoiling the world as we go.
We have had frigid winters, drought, oil spills, and global warm-
ing, all preapocalyptic events in nature that remind us of the fragile
character of our habitat. From the 1972 Stockholm Environment
Conference to the 1994 Rome Conference on Population and
Ecology, we have seen exhibited a markedly gentler spirit, empha-
sizing our need for humility in our management of nature.[2]

At the personal level, youth in particular lead our culture into
new depth and height awareness.[3] This total spectrum of evidence
signals a profound cultural change. One might suggest, with
Charles Reich, that technology is at least making a necessary
response to its own self-destructive tendencies.[4] Alternatively, we
might interpret these crises as the human quest for the roots of
our technological consciousness. We may indeed be searching for
the deep meanings of the reason we became technological, to be
able to decide whether and how we should go on. We celebrate
the liberating and humanizing impulses of modern Western civilization. We decry the dominations and oppressions of those same

9

cultures. Knowledge of roots can help contour appropriate dreams by discerning and celebrating cultural goods and discarding cultural evils. The discovery of these roots, we hope, will help us to establish value in the world we are creating.

In our technical genius, we have transformed nature and time into an environment in which we now find ourselves alienated. We live, work, eat, travel, and sleep among our own fabrications. We accelerate time in our industry, education, and even leisure, so that we are enslaved by the momentum. We probe the macrocosmos with the likes of *Voyager* and the space shuttles, and explore the microcosmos in molecular biogenetics and the human genome project, yet our own self lies unexplored in the twilight zone between. Now, because of the deepening mystery of human being, of our own self, the haunting questions why, where, and to what purpose keep crying out.

This book attempts to search back through the pathways of technological consciousness to discern those insights that might serve not only to sustain enduring meaning in life but also to guide us in the tasks of technological assessment and planning. We will seek to weave a thread of causality and conscience from operative normative axioms back to the hopes and ways of looking at the world that first gave rise to those values. We are on a quest to save life and secure health. This is a moral quest, in which both technical and cultural streams flow from underlying spiritual ethical springs.

Although the issues of biotechnology are closest to my interest, they symbolize the larger technical realm where humans transform matter and energy. One problem we will consider, for example, is the current upsurge of apocalyptic and catastrophic imagery used to describe the environmental crisis (Meadows, Forrester).[5] Human life in the world more generally is viewed in this way as fundamentalist faiths intensify. These widely discussed opinions regarding the endurability of humanity on the earth and the earth's carrying capacity can be traced to the apocalyptic roots of technical consciousness, and they can be evaluated in terms of the ethical elements of that consciousness—namely, apocalyptic creativity and discontent.

My thesis is very simple. If only we listen *care*-fully (I use this word precisely) to the rational and volitional wisdom that first evoked the technical act from human consciousness, we will discover those ethical insights sufficient to save and guide us. My arguments are based on an understanding of reality within which humans are imbued with ethical insight sufficient to each technical challenge. Both time and space, as Whitehead has shown, are structures of human moral intelligence, mediating intuitive norms. What we value is adequate to guide the use of what we make. This insight, I will contend, is implicit in the human act of knowledge and creation. Humans, of course, can choose to appropriate or neglect this insight, fulfilling or distorting the technical act, affirming or destroying our possibility. The human mind is imbued with structures of consciousness and conscientiousness sufficient to overcome propensities toward ignorance and violence, and to achieve moral wisdom.

In the modern world, the scientific and ethical components of human consciousness are united in an expression of technology. Humans *create* that which they value. In the advanced technological world, the creative act itself becomes value as the time lag between scientific thought and technological application collapses. For instance, Marconi's antennae in 1896 gave practical form to Maxwell's electromagnetic theory of 1869. But only six years lapsed between Otto Hahn's theory of nuclear fission and the atomic bomb. In the Manhattan Project, theoretical physicists built the bomb. Today knowledge and technology are simultaneous acts. Often, the theoretician and the technologist are the same person, and the design becomes the end product. *We* now reap what *we* sow. We cannot blame those who have gone before or harm future others by presumed delayed-effect.

The ethical import of this fact is reflected in Aristotle's famous statement that slavery would become unnecessary when weavers' shuttles could run by themselves. Technology takes scientific theory and fashions practical inventions to achieve human purposes. These purposes seek to actualize social values that may be destructive, defensive, or creative. In any case, they are values that express what, to some group, is desirable. If the thesis seems optimistic in this day of Bosnia, Rwanda, and germ warfare, let me assure the reader that I argue from the Christian doctrine of sufficient grace, not from benevolent human ingenuity.

Many contend that our ethical wisdom is not synchronized with our technical capacity. One Rabbi asked, "Are we wise enough to be so smart?" Utopianists argue that our knowledge of the good is far in advance of our achievement. Pessimists bemoan a terrible lag. I want to argue in Hegelian terms that human ethical consciousness does not lag or excel our technical capacity. It is concurrent and concomitant, and we remain fully responsible. We can know and will the good through our most sophisticated technological act. Otherwise, one must say that the rational intellect and technical creativity with which we are endowed is either a cruel hoax or an instrument of some malevolent spirit.

An example from the world of business: A major crisis in the Western world today is the downsizing of corporations in order to remain globally competitive. My thesis would hold that markets and products must be brought to coincide with resources: human and raw material. To exploit either producer or consumer is injustice that will destroy the enterprise itself.

This might be called an essay in natural theology, chastened with a small dose of Barthianism. I simply want to argue that when humans make something, they do so from a consciousness consisting of knowledge and technology; and this consciousness is competent to discern both the evil and the good. The will to do or not to do the good is another matter.

Even if this ambitious and highly elusive thesis cannot be established, it is absolutely certain that the values which technology was initially created to serve (e.g., automobiles for mobility, respirators for temporary pulmonic crises) are now threatened by those very technological processes. If those originating values can be recovered, perhaps the human quest constituted by human needs, hopes, sentiments, and the common good can be brought again to coincide with our technological venture. If the coincidence is not recovered, like the sorcerer's apprentice, our creation will destroy us.

When one attempts to understand technology in a normative frame, particularly one so basic as the human quest, one is beset by profound difficulties. Definitions are important at the outset. What is technology? Technology can be as specified as Microsoft Windows 95 or as elusive as Jacques Ellul's analysis of Technique. By *technology*, I refer to *the human process of making something new after the intellectual and scientific tasks of discovering and naming reality have occurred.* Faust enters the moral sphere only when, with Mephistopheles, he chooses to manipulate through his knowledge and power. It is application or utilization that sweeps technology into the normative sphere.

The human quest refers to that effort by humans to live with meaning and creativity as we adapt the environment to our needs and dreams. *Religiomedici* is Dr. Thomas Browne's caption for the cache of beliefs, values, and hopes that animate the enterprise of seeking life and health. I have deliberately chosen the word *quest* or adventure to reflect that healthy balance between conquest and fantasy within our hope. This venture at once expresses our noblest values and finest skills. I also use the word *quest* with Don Quixote de la Mancha in mind. In this context, it symbolizes an important clarification that must be made from the point of view of human psychodynamics. Where do fact and fantasy meet? We will return to this point after noting one additional problem: How do ethics square with experience? How do the things we create bear moral value?

One error in ethics is to allow technological values to become normative. Numerous critiques point up this accommodation.[6] Some critics suggest that decision-making in the elite technocratic mode is becoming the dominant style of value formation in our time. When the cigarette corporation threatens the television company with a $10 billion lawsuit, even the media giant backs down. Freedom of the press, a crucial rector of value in our culture, is vitiated. This validates the indictment of Noam Chomsky that corporate power ultimately drives human decisions. "Big Science" and scientific policy formulated by industry often succumb to this danger. Fortunately, many industrial concerns are coming to see that the relevant factors in technology assessment and planning go beyond cost-benefit analysis.

Another style of interface between values and technology that might simply be called pietism is a posture of withdrawal that often joins hands with the first attitude of accommodation. This position attributes an autonomy to both the technological and the value spheres. The mentality is very common among scientists, engineers, and technologists who cannot seem to apply the rigorous scientific analysis of their technical work to the area of faith and ethics. This group is joined by that multitude of frightened, simple folk who find no way to understand, let alone steer and control "big technology."

This attitude, which I label pietistic, even though it is frequently nonreligious, fails to realize the power of technology. It argues either that in the ultimate scheme of things, technology is inconsequential, or that it is an autonomous, uncontrollable force. There is a kind of naive religious optimism or diabolical fear, which in both cases leads to a "hands off" attitude. A Texas doctor wrote the following letter to me after reading our book *To Create a Different Future:*[7]

> Oh ye of little faith, solvers of the riddles of the universe, prophets of impending doom, drawers of maps and bell curves, sociological probers, psychological chroniclers, snatchers of hearts, hopers of hope, garblers of theology, and sons of god who dream of satan, worry not for the tomorrow for the morrow is sufficient unto itself.

Despite this disclaimer, technology's influence is profound and pervasive. "Science and technology," says Leiden medical Dean P. J. Thung, "recreate the world and our life. This not only because they have an exterior, instrumental influence, but because essentially they act from the inside out, constituting reality."[8]

From the perspective of a theological understanding, both the accommodating and the pietistic modes of value input are scientifically and ethically unfortunate. In the light of creation and redemption, we are caught up with God as cooperator in the process of change and transformation. "[We ourselves are] part of the 'technological world' which as the Cooperator Dei [God], must continue to share in creating."[9]

The only alternative to the state of affairs where people's values and the technological process are divorced is an enlightened mechanism of science policy. Such policy will include not only evaluation but planning and forecasting. It will involve the meaningful participation of all segments of society and will attend the global-social and ethical factors that override and often contradict the norms of expediency and even popular will.

Let us briefly return to the psychodynamics of hope and illusion. In Dale Wasserman's play *Man of La Mancha*, Don Quixote's dream transforms the barmaid Ladonza into the enchanting Dulcinea. By his illusory and irrational quest (the unreachable star, unrightable wrong, impossible dream), he fashions a world of beauty and love. He does this over against the rational-empirical constriction of "the Knight of Mirrors." He claims boldly that facts are the enemy of truth. The play asks how we are to distinguish between vision and illusion.

Throughout history, humans have imagined personal or social utopias that are fashioned out of both our hope and our disillusionment. We are being asked today to project utopias. The voluminous literature on hope in theology and futurology attests to the interface of technical and ethical consciousness.[10] Certainly, technics can be viewed as growing out of illusion—or even malice, as monumental and prideful assertion is behind the human quest—for instance, in military or espionage technology. Behind the technical evolution of the past two centuries, says Emil Brunner in his Gifford Lectures,

> there is a much deeper spiritual process. Modern technics is the product of the person who wants to redeem him/herself by rising above nature, who wants to gather life into his/her hand, who wants to owe his/her existence to nobody but him/herself, who wants to create an artificial world which is entirely his/her creation.[11]

When one reads the proposals to cover New York City with a geodesic dome or to construct a colony on the moon, one feels the power of Brunner's point. Humans have used, and will continue to use, technology as a cosmic instrument of anger and self-denial. Berdyaev, in *The Meaning of History*, spoke of the phase of history, following an epoch of order and synthesis, when continuing crisis creates inter-intrapersonal chaos. Humans feel detached from their worth, their work, even their selves. Religious movements based on self-annihilation gain strength. Here in the schism of the soul is born speculation, ranging from utopias and Armageddons to futures-games. Historian Martin Marty reflects that "this investment in the future can be read as a sign of restlessness, of neurotic anxiety on the part of people who have given up on complexity. . . . It may be the sick attempt to escape from history." [12]

Certainly the "fascination with things" characteristic of the psyche enamored with technology, and the obsessive future investment of those frightened by the terror of the present is a factor in the technological impulse. Mircea Eliade has noted that the quest for paradise and utopia is marked by a longing for primordial history (silent, unambiguous, undifferentiated) and a desire for new values and structures: "the hope for a radical *renovatio*." [13] The split within us between the destructive and the creative is implicit in technological consciousness, as it is in all aspects of our being. Although it may be pointed out that technological compulsion may be the expression of malice or even madness, one must remember that human creativity often emerges from such psychodynamic distortion. Even a realist like Reinhold Niebuhr accepts the transforming power of "The Impossible Dream." Speaking of the dream of justice, he writes:

> In the task of that redemption (of the total human enterprise) the most effective agents will be [those] who have substituted some new illusions for the abandoned ones. . . . Nothing but such madness will do battle with malignant power and "spiritual wickedness in high places." The illusion is dangerous because it encourages terrible fanaticisms. It must therefore be brought under the control of reason. One can only hope that reason will not destroy it before its work is done. [14]

Ernst Bloch has reminded us that the human quest is irresistibly drawn toward that desired future as it pursues those symbols of longing that make human consciousness what it is. If this is so, then our second problem, that of relating future to action, is not insurmountable. Humans reflect the full range of our will in technical action and evaluation of that action. It may be escape, illusion, or even madness, but it is madness without which our being withers and dies.

Technical and ethical insight emerge together: If we carefully scrutinize our technical consciousness, we will discover normative insight. Ethical insight can perceive the good; aesthetic insight, the beautiful; rational insight, the true. Being fashioned in the divine image, we can look on what we have made and say, "It is good." The challenge to technological humanity is to develop sufficient ascetic and mystic grace to see and hear, and thus discern value in the midst of technical enterprise.

I first will try to show the characteristics of the human quest for life and health. Then the main argument will be developed in the following steps. First, the roots of technological consciousness will be established in the Hebrew view of time, the Greek view of nature, the apocalyptic view of history, and the Christian view of the future. From these roots, we will derive principles of technology assessment and planning, which we will call axioms. The Hebrew understanding of time enables us to understand progress and technological acceleration. The Greek view of nature shows us the parameters of technological possibility by disclosing the wisdom of the ethical principles of creativity and discontent that are implicit in Nature and the apocalyptic consciousness. Finally, symbols of desired utopia and the commensurate technical imperatives can be located in the development of the Christic Eschatological mind.

In his Hasidic tales, Martin Buber tells of a hardened secularist student who proudly told the old Rabbi that he could not believe any longer. As the young man departed, the Rabbi quietly asked, "What if . . . God is?" The *Schreckliche Wieleicht* (the terrifying perhaps) is the projected question of this book.

The effort, of course, is grandiose and presumptuous. A theologian should more safely labor on some specific historical or analytical task. I confess that I am infected with the penchant that won our University of Chicago colleague, William McNeill, the 1996 Erasmus prize: "big history." I feel, however, that such effort is justified by the best traditions of systematic and constructive theology, the relevant traditions of ethics, and the urgent need for such exploration, however tentative, in our culture. The reader is given only hints and guideposts of paths toward a solution. The book is written for laypersons who seek to anchor their projects in the world, especially those who seek and serve human well-being, in an ethical framework. The author hopes it will assist those who seek to preserve and perpetuate value in our world.

CHAPTER ONE

The Hope for Well-Being and the Goals of Medicine

Let us now put some flesh on these bones. How does the concrete human quest of achieving healthful well-being reflect the impulses we have noted? The grand quest of medicine, especially in its Western (Europe, America, Israel, Japan, South Africa, etc.) version, is constituted by a thousand proximate goals. The ambitions and limitations, hopes and dreads that infuse this collective cultural psyche create a cache of concrete values. These include the goals of not being chained by the necessity of intercourse leading to conception and child bearing; of being born free from devastating genetic disease such as Tay-Sachs, sickle-cell anemia, or Downs syndrome; of transacting the birth process free from trauma and disease, respiratory distress, hyaline-membrane disease; of surviving childhood and youth without the lethal visitation of polio, malaria, or failure to thrive; of achieving adulthood without the crippling effects of cancer, heart, and blood-vessel disease; of securing old age without the devastations of mental illness, senility, and degenerative disease; of dying without the indignities of acute and prolonged suffering. These proximate goals together comprise a grand human hope that is unarticulated, perhaps even subconscious—namely, the hope for release from burdens of disease, debilitation, and death, and the yearning for total well-being.

What is the source of this hope for well-being? Beyond the survival instinct that we share with the animals, we can identify three roots: one scientific, one cultural, one moral. Unbounded optimism is released in the spirit of science and technology. Molecular biology and psychology—the human sciences—together with the earth and space sciences, have given human beings new knowledge and control to protect our lives from destruction, to accomplish many of our noblest purposes, and to overcome many of what once were thought to be the tragic necessities of nature.

Technology has given us techniques to better our life through sanitation, water purification, vaccination, scientific agriculture, and energy technology. The knowledge we are accumulating gives a great impetus to our hope.

Another root of our hope is sociocultural. We have a sense of time as a line of progress and pursuit of God's kingdom within the earth. This is the legacy of Judaism and Christianity. Whitehead acknowledged this source to be the major impulse to scientific and technical advance in the modern world.

> Science can rise only from the medieval insistence on the rationality of God, conceived as with the personal energy of Jehovah and the rationality of a Greek philosopher.[1]

It is this impulse that prompted the Benedictines to fashion new systems of agriculture and industry. It is this way of looking at the world that gave Galileo, Newton, Mendel, and Einstein the sense of development and breakthrough in knowledge. Thomas Kuhn talked of the great culminations of breakthroughs in knowledge and our expectant readiness. Einstein put it this way: "The

Lord God may be subtle but [God] isn't just plain mean" *(Böshaft ist er nicht)*.

Every mountain ascended by scientific inquiry only reveals another mountain before you. But you know that you will never have to climb this mountain again. In biomedicine, our cultural history yields a sense of progressive illumination as we confront the enigmatic realm of human disease. We can begin to hope, with pioneer heart surgeon Dr. Michael DeBakey, that science and technology will lead to breakthroughs in health, fostering longer and fuller lives, released from the ancient scourges of disease and disability.[2]

"American technology," said *U.S. News and World Report*, "promises to add new dimensions to the well-being of humankind in times ahead. . . . Ways to cure and prevent most forms of two major killers—cancer and heart disease—are within reach, and creation of life in a test tube would become routine."[3] In addition to this intellectual root of our hope pushing us forward because of what we can discover and understand, and the historiocultural root encouraging us to dream of what we could create, there is also a moral root that challenges us with the sense of what we *should* do.

"The plague is the will of God," intoned the Renaissance preachers. "I'm not so sure!" cried the skeptics in the spirit of Camus. There may be bacilli and fleas and rats and this rotten water supply. Speaking of yellow fever in ancient Rome, Noah Webster writes:

> Whenever a plague broke out, their priests consulted the oracles and Sibylline books for directions on how to check the disease, and both at Rome and Athens, when they found that their prayers to their gods were unavailing to arrest the disorder, they abandoned their devotion and gave themselves up to every species of immorality.
>
> While I avow myself a firm believer in the being and perfections of a God, I freely declare that I do not believe that being ever did or will interpose a miraculous power, to change the laws of nature and prevent disease, in places where its natural causes exist. I do not believe that almighty power will be exerted in a special way to cleanse dirty streets and cellars, or to save people who wallow in filth, intemperance and debauchery, from falling victims to fever.[4]

A mood of moral indignation and corrective action is part of the hopeful spirit: indignation at misery caused by man's harmful actions or failures to act. Robert Morrison has shown how John Wesley stimulated the modern era of public health by condemning filth and human squalor, because when viewed over against the divine perfection intended for humankind, such degradation was intolerable. Cleanliness was next to godliness. Moltmann drives to the eschatological heartbeat of this vitality:

> Those who hope (in Christ) can no longer put up with reality as it is, but begin to suffer under it to contradict it. Peace with God means conflict with the world, for the goad of the promised future stabs inexorably into the flesh of every unfulfilled present.[5]

This chapter will distill the essence of the several moods of belief and value that we have identified from our ethical heritage. These epochal insights, which will be briefly illustrated by biomedical examples, will then be elaborated in subsequent chapters.

The Hebrews

Matthew Arnold often spoke of Israel as the nation that knew the way the world was going. For the Hebrew, Yahweh is the Maker of all. God is the breath of human life. God is the righteous judge of history. God sustains nature. God fashions space and activates time. God leads the chosen people through suffering to the land of promise. God demands righteousness. The idea of linear time and progress are born in this faith. So is our concept of human stewardship over life and the garden. The notion that the Divine will would establish a global community where peace and justice reign is a theme of Hebrew philosophy drawn from many precursor and cognate faiths. The important ethical derivatives of this tradition concern respect for persons, care of the earth, affirmations of an open time horizon, a passion for righteousness, and the shalom of the Lord in the earth.

The Greeks

The Greeks discern the continuities of humankind and nature, and find them good. Human reason is structured to understand reality. There are boundaries in nature which, when understood and accepted, bring contentment and fulfillment. The noblest hope is conformation; know thyself, accept fate, honor one and all.

The Apocalypticists

As classic culture collapsed, a new way of looking at things emerged—a way we might call apocalyptic. Here hope and discontent are intensified. The old order is being shaken and dismantled. A new reality is being revealed. The earth quakes, the heavens are torn, the new age dawns. Apocalyptic consciousness still shapes our hope. Apocalypse is awaited in time and space, history and nature. It activates two millennia of revolutions. It prompts millennial visions and utopian expectations. Newton and Da Vinci found it at the center of the enterprise of science and technology. Here our mood of impatience is born, along with an active pursuit of vision and resistance against impediments to that vision.

The Christians

The New Testament and the Christian Church were born in the period of Jewish apocalyptic. Several elements of this new way of perceiving reality are crucial to the hope for life and health that we have inherited from that faith. The new covenant continues the anti-idolatrous or iconoclastic task of the old—of stripping the world of its demonic hold, of disenchanting nature, of desacralizing the world. Humans can now move within and against nature without fear. The world can be perceived objectively, instrumentally, and experimentally. Here, of course, we find the roots of secularization and enlightenment, which only recently has degenerated into positivism and materialism. These deteriorations come more from the spirit of atheistic humanism than from the biblical tradition.

The hope of the Christian is gathered in a Christology that sees Jesus as the Lord, the *Kosmokrator* in the spirit of the Greek fathers, John's Gospel, Colossians, and to some extent, the book of Hebrews. The God-person is the one through whom and for whom the universe exists. Energies are now recognized within nature, and especially within the community—energies that are called spiritual. These are foretastes of the kingdom of God. These new resources are seen to be healing, reconciling, integrating; they can mend together brokenness. Under the influence of Greek philosophy, humanity is seen to be spirit—not in the Hebrew sense of being "inbreathed," but in the sense of possessing an immortal soul. This experience of a new quality of life activates an anticipation for a total regeneration and transformation, or transmutation, of the world. This hope prompts active waiting, sometimes revolution, sometimes the lust for apocalypse, sometimes a slow and careful desire to build the earth.

In the normative center of this tradition, persons, and the collective human family are precious. The human response to a love that went to a cross is to care for all, especially the sick, the vulnerable, the outcast, the weak, the least of these.

We have inherited the legacy of Judaism and Christianity, intensified by apocalyptic, contoured by Greek naturalism. How does this hope, this quest for well-being that is bounded by certain sensibilities, correlate with the goals of modern medicine? How does this analysis help us, in this day when the energies of discovery and conquest are tempered—some say dampened—by the mood of reflection and resignation? We live in a day when the federal government has declared a moratorium on fetal research and DNA recombination, and is seriously reflecting on the ethical dimensions of behavioral and biomedical investigations. It is a day when grants for research on the human genome include ethics projects. It is a day when abortion clinics are bombed, and doctors who have performed abortions are killed. It is a day when synagogues are stations for Tay-Sachs screening, and genetic disease is being compared to communicable disease. We have declared a war on cancer and blood-vessel disease. It is a day when the fear of the cost of getting sick is making many people sick. It is a day when some feel that they must write a living will so that they will be allowed to die. It is a day when Dr. Kevorkian dispatches persons from death machines in his Volkswagen bus.

How do the goals of today's medicine contrast with the hope that brought them into being in the first place? We can speak of four functions that medicine is being asked to perform in society. These functions are in concord or discord with the underlying moral symphony in the four movements we are offering in this book.

We ask medicine to have a *preventive* function. We want to know what causes sickness and how it runs its course. Where possible, we want it prevented. The air- and water-borne infectious diseases were attacked at both levels—polio and malaria were overcome when the environmental causes were eliminated and the preventive immunizations introduced. We are now asking medicine, or better, the public-health service, to prevent birth defects. We will soon screen for genetic and congenital defects. Parents will not knowingly give birth to defective children, nor will society allow them to, if it must pay the bill. In natality practice today, we have the strange paradox of "mail-order kids" among the affluent and lingering infant-wastage among the poor. Even the most basic function of medicine, *prevention*, is ambivalent today.

Another function medicine performs might be called *corrective*. Children are tested for PKU disease at birth, and the required therapy is begun where indicated. The diabetic is treated with insulin. Minor and major birth defects are surgically corrected. We attempt to excise, or at least halt, the spread of cancer. When the vascular system becomes diseased, we try to reroute critical vessels or put in synthetic ones. Much of medicine is an activity similar to maintaining a house. The body weathers. It needs constant upkeep. Psychiatry and counseling are essentially corrective medicine. The interventions are designed to restore balance, equilibrium, and function. The great majority of efforts in corrective medicine fall within the contours of the values of well-being provoked by our hope. Questions may arise when correcting becomes rebuilding and refashioning.

Remodeling is a third function we ask medicine to perform. Plastic surgery for aesthetic reasons—skin tightening, bust building, orthodontics, and the like are major industries. Though these touch-up jobs are not nearly as questionable as more basic designs to make "better" people, they still may be peripheral purposes for medicine (Leon Kass). Geneticists, prompted by a value that on first reading sounds good—that all children have the right to be born normal (Bentley Glass)—urge us to plan mating, perhaps use unnatural modes of fertilization and gestation to make better babies.[6] Some advocate an era of cyborg medicine, where we rebuild persons with a variety of artificial parts, organs, or limbs. Most of us are in one way or another prosthetic people; at least, most of our mouths have been rebuilt and our eyes augmented. Some behavioral therapists hold out to us the promise of transforming epileptic fits into controlled episodes, to turn us on from frigidity with happy buttons, to transform aggression into sweetness. Some few individuals now departed are not really deceased—they are merely "cooling it" in liquid nitrogen capsules until they can be cured. (Curing, incidentally, is a good word if any of you have ever eaten hickory-smoked bacon.) With all the positive value in this area, we might find an inordinate longing, one not appropriate to our hope, a desire that we might wish to question.

There is a further degradation of medical purpose. The fourth goal should not need to be mentioned in a civilized society. But we must identify it. Medicine has sometimes been called to perform *retaliative*, or destructive purposes. The most benign form of this can sneak up on us and perhaps delude us into thinking it benevolent. Some years ago a poster of a wanted criminal with a rare skin disorder was printed in the *Journal of the American Medical Association Archives of Dermatology* (February 1972). "If you see this man in your office," it asked, "please inform the FBI." The leading journal of the American Dental Association printed the record of Patty Hearst's teeth, indicating her next dental needs that would bring her to a dentist's office.

Fortunately, despite the noble patriotism of the professions of both dermatology and dentistry, a few have rejected the political use of their caring arts. Yet both posters were printed. One African state still requires its doctors to execute the government's will to punish stealing with the amputation of an arm. American doctors have been asked to administer lethal injection in capital punishment. Politicians in many nations make economic judgments that are euthanasic—deciding who will live and who will die through budget decisions. The more subtle and significant issues arise when medicine is called to fulfill the malignant purpose of the state turned against human values. The Nazi physicians practiced what the Nuremberg trials called ktenology, the art of killing the undesirable. Some say that we are returning to this gate of hell. Cancer and heart treatments for the poor in inner cities are inferior to those offered in suburbia. Is this euthanasia? Even if we are not so degraded, we do need to be cautious, especially in our mass society, inclined toward expediency, equipped with technological instrumentation and possessing a blunted conscience.

We have mentioned the preventing, correcting, remodeling, and retaliating purposes that occupy medicine. The goals of medicine, for the most part, flow from a good intent; they are appropriately anchored in our hopeful ethos. Several concluding reflections might serve to restore medicine, or keep medicine, if you like, to its appropriate task.

First, we should attempt to balance the commitment to the experimental and exotic treatments with the commitment to universalize what we now can do. Heart, kidney, and liver transplants are completely justified, if we are motivated to one day make these available to all who need them, provided they prove successful. But why should dialysis and kidney transplantation be guaranteed to all under Social Security, when well-baby care, for example, is not? In this regard, should not the national and international commitment be as strong to the primary and secondary health-delivery services as they now are to the tertiary research and specialized-care centers? We will need incentives such as Russia and European commonwealths have used to distribute competent health personnel equitably across this network.

The second point is very subtle. Medicine should be concerned with relieving pain, not obliterating suffering. Abolition of suffering is not a realistic goal. We are a pill-popping culture, with a very low threshold for pain. We have fashioned a global drug network, consume mountains of Valium and cigarettes, then scapegoat athletes with marijuana testing. We find more and more ways to anesthetize ourselves, from both the signals of discord in our own bodies and the signals of despair from the world around us. Our typical response to suffering—famine, war, poverty, whatever pain it may be somewhere out there—is to turn on the television and light another cigarette. Suffering can be redemptive. It need not be. It can be devastating, destructive of our humanity. The new drugs that are specified and localized are a great benefit. But suffering will remain our lot. We must search out its meaning.

This leads to a final suggestion. Medicine should be concerned with protecting life's possibilities, rather than curing disease and fighting death. There is very likely a certain constant burden of disease and an absolutely constant burden of mortality that will endure in our imperfect world. We simply could describe all disease along a spectrum, with infectious disease at one end, degenerative disease and cancer in the middle, mental illness at the other end. In one sense, our effort only exchanges one disease for another; CDC now finds violence as the major kid-killer. If so, perhaps we should be less concerned with those that can destroy the body than with those that can destroy the soul. On the other hand, we may be coming strong out of that side of the spectrum and throwing disease ascendancy back to the plagues. Death itself, and its symbolic prefiguration, disease, signal to humans their destiny. We must accept our fragmentariness as prelude to our wholeness. We are condemned to die, and therefore born to love and trust. Perhaps a clue to this enigma is found in one of the most difficult verses in the New Testament: "The creation was subjected to futility, not of its own will but by the will of him who subjected it in hope" (Romans 8:20 RSV).

Surely, the goals of medicine should be to prevent the scourge of unnecessary disease; to restore our life from premature injury; to watch and guard with us during life's precarious pilgrimage; to accompany us with care to a good death; and to secure this well-being for each child of the earth.

"[We] can," says biologist Theodosius Dobzhansky, "make [our] existence something more than a 'passing whiff of insignificance.' [We] can, if we choose, contribute toward the achievement of a higher life for [ourselves] and for the world of which [we] are part."[7]

The struggle for life against death should finally yield peace. It does in Elisabeth Kübler-Ross' stages of dying. It does in the near-death literature. Loren Eisely said, "I think science more and more is going to be giving its attention to finding ways whereby humanity can lie at peace with itself and nature."[8] Perhaps Jürgen Moltmann is right: "Just because biomedical progress elicits hopes and yet does not contain a guarantee of happiness, it must be guided by a human ethic which ought to lead from the struggle for existence to peace in existence."[9]

The stage is now set to explore in depth the aforementioned sources of ethical insight. We have summarily sketched the characteristics of the quest for life and health, and the underlying value springs. To these momentous and formative features of our moral imagination, we now turn.

CHAPTER TWO

Formative Influences on Our Technological and Ethical Conscience

The Hebrew Understanding of Time as Linear

The deepest of Western, now global, technological consciousness, and a constant ethical vision, is located in the Hebrew understanding of time and history. Here Judeo-Christian world-consciousness and conscience has its origin. It is this tradition that gives birth to technology in its Western manifestation. We find impressive technology in old China and Egypt, among other cultures. But a unique worldview and spirit of progress and aggression verging on the irresistible emerges in the Christianized Roman Empire, the monastic culture, medieval Europe, the Renaissance-Reformation, through to the new appearing global technological village linked by the information highway. Although it is difficult to trace the threads from nineteenth- and twentieth-century science-based technology back through the Enlightenment, Renaissance, Rome and Greece to Israel, it is here that our story begins.

The Jewish understanding of time is encapsulated in the historical confession recorded in Deuteronomy: A wandering Aramean was my father; and he went

> down into Egypt and sojourned there, few in number; and there he became a nation, great, mighty, and populous. And the Egyptians treated us harshly, and afflicted us, and laid upon us hard bondage. Then we cried to Yahweh the God of our fathers, and Yahweh heard our voice, and saw our affliction, our toil, and our oppression; and Yahweh brought us out of Egypt with a mighty hand and an outstretched arm, with great terror, with signs and wonders; and he brought us into this place and gave us this land, a land flowing with milk and honey.
>
> Deuteronomy 26:5b-9 RSV

I t is all there—the full understanding of humanity, world, history, and God. Humans are now hopers, strivers, builders, inquirers. Humankind comes to conceive its destiny as a journey. Not that these elements did not appear before. High technical creativity surfaced previously in the Orient, the Mediterranean isles, and North Africa. A dozen dynasties and Hesiod's Gold and Silver Ages had already passed when the inchoate peoples to become the nation Israel appeared in Egypt. Yet it is here that those understandings of God and nature, influenced by many precedents, are set in sharp relief, indeed radically innovated, so that a new consciousness could emerge.

Monotheism was not new. The Egyptian deities, as well as the Indo-European sky-god, represent a theology that anticipated Hebrew monotheism. It is the element of direction or intentionality that is important in the new consciousness; technical and ethical consciousness are joined in a unique way in the Hebrew mentality.

The elements of this consciousness can be extracted from the confession cited above. They concern humans as active creative human beings, living in a world possessed and directed by God, to whom they are responsible.

Yahweh creates nature in time. Days mark the creation. The

Hebrew recognizes Yahweh as the sovereign power over time and natural events. The Exodus is a leading out and forward by God: a release and a new possibility. Ernst Bloch has shown in a forceful way how Israel's desert rendezvous with the God of Exodus marks the end of religion:

> Religion is re-ligio, binding back. It binds its adherents back, first and foremost, to a mythical God of the Beginning, a Creator-God. So rightly understood, *adherence* to the Exodus-figure called "I will be what I will be," and to the Christianity of the Son of Man and the Eschaton is no longer religion.[1]

The power of God is manifest in natural events, full of terror, yet indicative of God's direction. Nature bears Yahweh's judgment and grace. The terror of the wilderness is followed by the bountiful land "flowing with milk and honey."

The earliest Hebrew historian to understand the meaning of time wrote in the tenth century B.C., probably during the time of Solomon. We call him or her J (Jahwist) because Yahweh is used as the divine name. The author weaves memories from the prehistoric consciousness (the creation, fall, first family, etc.) together with insights of other traditions, into present events to express Hebrew faith. Here God is understood as goodness despite the foolishness and pride of man. Yahweh executes sovereignty and power in the creation: the Flood, the confusion of languages. Time is understood as an allotment within which humanity can obey, respond, and accomplish destiny as God's creature. Time is the span wherein humankind is given something to be and something to do. In freedom, humans must decide personally and collectively whether or not to respond. And Abraham and his descendants claim this opportunity. After rebelling, arguing, complaining, and purging, they are led into the good land and promised prosperity and posterity. The land is a benediction to our faithfulness, or a curse on our neglect.

The great theologian who wrote Second Isaiah reaffirms this high lordship of God over the creation. God has fashioned all of our nature; therefore all creation acts responsively at God's Word. Nature is fashioned in time—God's time.

> Hear me, Jacob,
> and Israel whom I called:
> I am He; I am the first,
> I am the last also.
> With my own hands I founded the earth,
> with my right hand I formed the expanse of sky;
> when I summoned them,
> they sprang at once into being. . . .
> I am the LORD your God:
> I teach you for your own advantage
> and lead you in the way you must go.
> (Isaiah 48:12-13, 17*b* NEB).

In a similar vein, the priestly writing chastened by the exile stresses the divine ordering of nature and history with the powerful element of the indwelling presence of God among God's people, working peace and purpose (Genesis 17:6-8). The great assurance here is that the human hope for restoration and healing (Ezekiel) is now present among us in the living God. Eschatology, ethics, and technology are joined in unitive consciousness, as God's faithful presence in and with God's people prompts human perception of the "yet to be." This perception carries with it the responsibility for that possibility, and the mandate to act.

It is not a natural and necessary order, a cosmos, that Hebrew consciousness perceives. That would prove far too frail. Only in late Greek wisdom could consciousness rest on that discernment. Only the ultimate reality can sustain that parcel of reality that we know.

> The human of the Old Testament knows nothing of an order of nature, governed by law, comprehensible in terms of rational thought. But the human believes in a God who has created the world and given it into the charge of [humankind] as the place for [God's] dwelling and working.[2]

On the basis of this time-activated, divinely directed cosmology, the Hebrew mind understands the long momentum of history. Not only does the human quest and technical action place in this lively dynamic, it has meaning in terms of historical sequence. Because a creator-God is leading humanity and all nature to God's intended goal, history comes to be understood as divided into segments, each having a purpose in the divine progression. History is a unity constituted by successive events directed along a line from creation to consummation. Hebrew consciousness expects perfection or restoration of reality, because time has a beginning and a continuity. For the Hebrew mind, creation is not yet complete; it is becoming. It is going on. "I am doing a new thing . . . do you not perceive it?" (Isaiah 43:19 RSV). Sometimes the process is seen as redemptive. Here the emphasis is the creation of something new or the healing of something broken. Sometimes the new is judgment, undoing and dismantling. Sometimes it is symbolized as some *magna restoratio* (F. Bacon). Sometimes the future is perceived as a return to a distant past.

This notion has powerful technological significance, as will be seen as our argument unfolds. If nature, yet imperfect, is being redeemed or restored, then we have ambivalent responsibility in our technical act. On the one hand, we are responsible for the imperfection and the fault: therefore we are called to correct the fault. On the other hand, we are invited to cooperate in the renewing task. Most Western understandings of ethical ambivalence, I would contend, can be understood only against the backdrop of this Hebrew consciousness.

What one author calls "retro-historical consciousness" in ancient Israel is important to note at this point.[3] This Spirit-consciousness evokes present norms—for example, the Decalogue; and from norms of the eternal past—for example, Moses. Today's values are not constructions or precepts of plurality, but are anchored in the creation of reality. Thus Hebrew human beings remember as they hope. They long for and work for the Kingdom that was and therefore will be (Isaiah 11:6-9; Joel 3:9ff.). This is more than what René Dubos relates as the nostalgic "golden age" consciousness, where humans fantasize a paradise behind or beyond the present desperation.[4] The Hebrew mind knows that nature is wholesome and incorruptible because she comes from the hand of the same righteous Lord that Israel meets in her life events. This secret of nature, this paradise, was and will be, and we must participate in that recovery.

Hebrew consciousness of time, in its natural and historical aspect, has three implications for technology. The notion of the righteousness of God initially amplifies this understanding of time. It is on this point that the whole energy of the Hebrew insight focuses. God is just and good. Therefore humans, in their being and action, must meet the demands of righteousness. Technical power has one purpose: the achievement of goodness, the eradication of injustice, the accomplishment of peace, *shalom.*

Here again we are confronted with an insight that antedates Judaism. The understanding of God as the fount of justice is fundamental to human religious consciousness. "It is quite inappropriate," says W. F. Albright, "to ask, how did the God of nature become the God of ethics in Israel?—because the god of nature was also lord of ethics from remote pre-Israelite times. In Assyria and Babylon, the sun-god was also the patron of justice, and there was a similar relation in the case of all high gods."[5] Yet it is Hebrew wisdom that anchors ethical reality in nature and in God. God is defined by justice, justice by God. Justice is not the capricious will of the gods, nor is it the graceless necessity of fate. Justice is and justice will be, because God is Lord of creation and the maker of humankind. Justice has a particular meaning in Judaism. It means both purity of devotion and coincidence of will. The first danger Israel faces upon entering Canaan is contamination. The ascetic ideal of a pure heart is the rudimental requirement of justice. When Israel's passion sways to other gods, her actions also diverge from God's will, and her misdirection becomes her sin. Idolatry is misspent or misdirected energy and creativity. Her will no longer coincides with Yahweh's. Time and again Israel's disaster follows her impurity.

To give this point modern illustration, we might say that a Jew cannot divorce will from action. A Jew cannot say with the Nazi technician: "I was only following orders." The Germans forsook their Judeo-Christian heritage when they drew this cleavage between intention and technical act. A most brilliant treatment of the psychic impossibility of this splitting (Lifton) is Albert Speer's *Inside the Third Reich.* In this memoir he records how as a young man he energetically assumed the technical tasks of building the

Reich architecture, then the *Wehrmacht*, without cognizance of the ethical import of his act. Only later were the motivations of conscience and action reunited in a terrifying perception. His closing words at the Nuremberg trial were these:

> Hitler's dictatorship was the first dictatorship of an industrial state in this age of modern technology, a dictatorship which employed to perfection the instruments of technology to dominate its own people. By means of such instruments of technology as the radio and public-address systems, eighty million persons could be made subject to the will of one individual. Telephone, Teletype, and radio made it possible to transmit the commands of the highest levels directly to the lowest organs where, because of their high authority, they were executed uncritically. Thus many officers and squads received their evil commands in this direct manner. The instruments of technology made it possible to maintain a close watch over all citizens and to keep criminal operations shrouded in a high degree of secrecy. To the outsider, this state apparatus may look like the seemingly wild tangle of cables in a telephone exchange; but like such an exchange, it could be directed by a single will. Dictatorships of the past needed assistants of high quality in the lower ranks of the leadership also— men who could think and act independently. The authoritarian system in the age of technology can do without such men. The means of communication alone enable it to mechanize the work of the lower leadership. Thus the type of uncritical receiver of orders is created.[6]

Only as humans become idolatrous and forsake the source of their consciousness can they separate ethics from technics. Only when they lose their humanity in contamination or false consciousness can they make this divorce. This is because technological humanity is Hebrew. In God, the consciousness is integrated.

Time in the Hebrew sense has an urgency, a character of crisis. It bears judgment. The prophets repeatedly speak of the Time of Reckoning when God will execute justice. Amos, for example, gives time this urgency:

> . . . prepare to meet thy God, O Israel. For, lo, he that formeth the mountains, and createth the wind, and declareth unto man what is his thought, that maketh the morning darkness, and treadeth upon

the high places of the earth, The LORD, The God of hosts, is his
name.

(Amos 4:12*b*-13 KJV)

The moral purpose of God has to do with the earth, according
to Hebrew faith. Just as nature mediates God's judgment, she is
controlled and renewed by God's grace. Nature is not destined to
terrifying death-throes in some *Götterdämmerung;* rather, she
waits expectantly for renewal as new heaven and new earth. Blessing accompanies God's justice, as together in time they work to
fulfill God's promise (Genesis 8:14–9:2). "Blessing" for the
Hebrew means responsibility, not evasion. Especially in the Age
of Technology is this Hebrew insight sharpened. Buckminster
Fuller states:

> The poor illiterate masses prayed . . . that they be blessed and pos-
> sibly escape by death from unendurable life to a dreamed-of good
> life thereafter. (Recall Orcagna's painting, "The Poor Invoking
> Death" Santa Croce Museum, Florence). All this is now changed
> . . . because we have found out what a few of the invisible principles
> operative in the physical universe can do. But the universe having
> permitted us to discover our intellectual (and technical) effective-
> ness as well as some of the universe's riches . . . will now require us
> to use intellect (and technology) directly and effectively. Success or
> failure is now all of humanity's responsibility.[7]

Humans live, work, and create; that is, they are *responsible*
within the enfolding justice of God. Therefore our technology is
swept into the same normative framework as our being and
action. Technology, as any human knowledge or skill, has the central purpose of fulfilling God's just and good will. We shall derive
middle axioms and practical implications of this understanding in
the later sections.

Hebrew consciousness understands creation as the linear-time
reality, created under the sovereignty of Yahweh. Our manipula-
tions with nature fall under the mark of Cain, the first technologist, as they proceed with a treacherous ambivalence under the
judgment of God.

A second implication of the Hebrew view of time concerns

eschatology. Two elements interplay in Hebrew thought. Both are present in the Hebrew Scripture. Although one view prevails, the other appears in Daniel and is enlarged in apocalyptic literature. In eschatological understanding, God goes before time and draws the present forward from the past. God is Lord of all time, because God draws each present moment from the past into God's future. The great Hebrew indicative, "I am who I am," more accurately stated "I will be what I will be" (Exodus 3:14) affirms this truth. The great contribution of Bergson, Heidegger, and Whitehead in philosophy, and Pannenberg in theology, is to incorporate the idea of time into the being of God. When Heidegger speaks of God as "infinite temporality," he invokes a return to the early Hebrew understanding.[8]

> The very essence of God implies Time. Only in the future of his Kingdom come will the statement, "God exists" prove to be definitely true. . . . In this impending power, the coming God was already the future of the remotest past. He was the future also of that "nothing" which preceded creation.[9]

Here again, human responsibility is emphasized. Because the power of the future is God, humans are responsible to strain toward that possibility with technical power and ethical awareness. The future is not an empty vacuum, nor is it an uncharted sea. The future is the reality of God.

A further Hebrew understanding of time that nourishes the roots of our technical consciousness is the notion that God approaches and contacts human life. This is a simple, yet profound and fundamental idea. Paul Tillich has noted the different ways Hebrew faith has articulated this contact: the *Shekinah* is the dwelling of God on earth; the *Memra*, the Word of God (later to unite with the Greek Logos in John's Gospel); the "Spirit of God." In addition, there are the divine intermediaries who traffic between God and humans.[10]

In Hebrew, and then Christian faith, God comes to people and dwells with them. This is the deep meaning of Emmanuel, of Bethlehem. While much has been made of the important notion of disenchantment of nature in Hebrew thought,[11] it must be balanced by the view that God's presence in history at once secularizes and sacralizes. Humans are released from those idolatrous understandings wherein humanity and all things are possessed with spirits and demons. This is the meaning of demythologizing in the Bible. Theologian W. F. Albright has swept away volumes of such shallow thought by noting that "the Bible already 'demythologizes' its source material by excising myths or by taking certain mythical elements in their corresponding empirical form, and using them in the service of a higher religious vision." [12] At the same time, this religious vision sees the world in which we now live as the sacred reality, because God the Lord, unconditioned by nature, ingratiates nature with God's presence. Mystical Judaism, particularly in its medieval expression, recaptures this sense of cosmic sacrality. [13]

Finally, history, or time in the Hebrew sense, is holy time. All history—even those most godforsaken moments—is God's time, God's history. The implication of this consciousness is that all history, as all nature, is ultimately sacred (Ricoeur). Therefore, this time, this temporality, is captured in an overarching purpose of the Creator. It therefore has more profound significance than present discernment allows, and deeper responsibility than a "que sera sera" mentality would prompt. Eliade shows the importance of this element for progress and responsibility: "For the first time, the prophets place a value on history, succeed in transcending the vision of the cycle, and discover a one-way time. . . . Historical facts thus became 'situations' of humanity with respect to God." [14]

Time is an element brought into our consciousness by the Old Testament prophets and the New Testament Gospels, says Emil Brunner:

> History is no circular movement. History is full of new things, because God works in it, the historical time process leads somewhere. . . . This is because God has entered this circular time at a certain point, and with God's whole weight of eternity has stretched out this time-circle and given the time-line a beginning and an end, and so a direction. By this incarnation or "intemporation" of the world of God, time has been charged with an immense intensity. [15]

The Hebrew sense of time, with its urgency, is released into Christian culture and there constitutes a fundamental aspect of both technical and ethical consciousness. But this consciousness is transmitted through the Hellenistic world and late Judaistic apocalyptic, to which we must now turn.

The Greek Concept of the Wisdom of Nature

If, in the Hebrew worldview, Yahweh has dramatically and demandingly entered history, for the Greeks the whole world is full of gods (Thales). From the enthusiastic mythology of the Olympian religion to the sublime heights of Platonic philosophy and Aristotelian science, all Greek consciousness sees nature infused and permeated with the divine. The world is the body of God. The soul or mind (*logos*) is the touchstone. On the surface, this might seem reason to reject the Greek period as one contributing to the emergence of technological consciousness. For decades, scholars have stressed the fact that a Parmenidean worldview, basic to Greek thought, is unable to initiate science and technology because of its static and cyclic character.[16] Others, like Alfred North Whitehead, have stressed the importance of the Greek legacy, particularly the medieval phase of Judeo-Christian tradition with the elements of rationality of nature and lineal tradition of progress. Whitehead, for example, organizes his great history of science in the modern world around the thesis that science can rise only from "the medieval insistence on the rationality of God, conceived as with the personal energy of Jehovah and with the rationality of a Greek philosopher."[17]

Recently, however, the Greek contribution to the consciousness that gave birth to science and technology has been reemphasized. Carl von Weizsäcker, whose early writing on secularization stressed the importance of the Hebrew-Christian element, now finds the Greek worldview to be far more determinative than he previously thought.[18] Regardless of the outcome of this debate, it is undeniable that the Greek mentality, in its physical, poetic, and metaphysical dimensions, has deeply informed Western consciousness.

In this section, we will seek to analyze this soil in which the roots of our technical and ethical consciousness are nurtured. Although the limits of this small book allow only highly suggestive description and analysis, we may note elements in Greek religion, philosophy, and science which may help us discern value in our subsequent technical applications.

The Greek Olympus is born in the "travail of the Mycenaean epoch." This great cultural upheaval released into the world a vision of reality that still runs deep in our consciousness. Little is known of the Cretan or Aegean pantheons, which precede that of classical Greece. It is certain that a profound transformation of consciousness occurred that enabled humans to perceive deity in human form. Previous religions depicted the god in natural or animal form. A unique contribution of the Greek mind is to abolish the animal shape of deity.[19] A rational worldview which makes technical process possible is anchored in this religious transition. "Having reduced the god myths of the human dimension to mangods," says John McHale, "a religio-mythical worldview is transformed to rational vision of the city."[20]

The early theogonies, written around the eighth century B.C.E. (concurrent with the kingly and prophetic history of Israel) and contained in the poetry of Homer and Hesiod, are our principal sources. The early tradition seems to combine two strains: an Indo-European tradition, within which Zeus is the sky-father, fuses with a Mediterranean tradition in which Demeter, as earth mother, begins the family of gods. In the later Orphic cosmogonies, one finds more refined thought regarding the subtleties of the gods, humankind, and nature.

From the vast and dark chaos, a fertile power appears in Gaea, the "deep-breasted earth" with gods who create day and night. Gaea continues creation, fashioning the stars and the natural world; then with her family, the Uranus group, the Titans and the world of divine and human beings are formed. After Chronos enters the creation with considerable intrigue, the Olympians begin their ascent with the birth of Zeus. From the Titans spring humankind. Prometheus and Pandora initiate the long pilgrimage of mastery and misery that is to mark the human story.

Several elements of the religious consciousness of Greece are important to our theme. Initially, we note that in the Greek perception of reality, the supernal spiritual forces are involved in the patterns of nature and in the affairs of humanity. With Demeter and Athena, the daughter of Zeus, fertility and fecundity are symbolized. Athena sets the courses of the stars and the seasons. She stands by humans in protection and is the sovereign over life and death. What a noble concept for the human mind to attain! In God's providence, not only the Hebrew mind but the Hellenic mind is made ready for "the fullness of time" (*Kairos*/Galatians 4:4). At this moment in history, it is made known to humanity who we are to be and what we are to do.

Whereas Chronos, expressing the chaotic and disorderly, swallows all his children, Zeus is the god of life. After a great struggle, he plunges Chronos to the depths of the earth and forces him to regurgitate the gods. Zeus subsequently defeats the Titans, the Giants, and Typhoeus as he tames the elements of the world. As Guerand writes, "The divine wisdom, regulator of the universe, imposed its will over these disorderly elements."[21] This insight that time and order (*chronos*) tame the infinite void (*chaos*) is one of the sublime insights of all the classical religions. Again in Amerindian religion, it is the great spirit that bridles and pushes back thundering chaos. In Hebrew faith, the wind of God (*Ruach Elohim*) hovers over the chaotic deep as the Lord, through word, calls cosmos from chaos.

Nature then expresses the balance, harmony, and order of supernatural perfection. This may be articulated as figments of Platonic ideals or strivings of Aristotelian entelechies. Greek mathematics, music, and theology are the disciplines by which time touches noumenal principles and relationships. Plato lectured on "mathematics and the good" in the presence of Aristotle and Xenophon. The harmonious balance of nature is expressed in the architecture of Greece during the golden age. If you view the Parthenon from a longitudinal perspective, you see the intricate balance of each column delicately arched, each having a unique line. The mathematical conceptualization and the technological fabrication of the human mind designs and creates in resonance with the harmonies of nature.

Although one finds this high emphasis placed on cosmos out of chaos, and order informing all of reality, it must be noted that the Greek view of natural process is essentially tragic. The gods play with human fate. With the exception of Helios, the god of light, all the meteorological gods are capricious. The gods of wind, sky, and sea are often associated with the moros and fates, the relentless forces of destiny that deceive, defeat, and destroy humanity. The relentless necessity in matter itself is also central to the Greek view of nature. Built on the early natural philosophy of the Ionians, that view states that nature is determined by the natural manifestations of four basic forces—fire, earth, water, and air. Whitehead goes so far as to say that this notion, combined with fatalism of the Athenian tragedians, Aeschylus, Sophocles, and Euripedes, forms the concept of nature in modern thought.[22] Natural process is governed by remorseless fatalistic necessity, in the early modern worldview that gives rise to modern science.

Principles of order in Greek mentality are principles of restraint and boundary. Nature is ordered by certain parameters. Although we may throw ourselves against them in titanic fury, we must finally succumb and obey. Moros, the son of the night, exerts power over all the gods as the harbinger of human destiny. Even when it is a matter of saving his son Sarpedon, whose death the fates had marked down, Zeus can only bow his head and allow destiny her course.

The boundedness of reality is expressed in the Greek neglect of the future. The future is hidden from mortals. The seer Tiresias is struck blind by Hera. Apollo, when presenting the gift of predicting the future to Cassandra, attaches to it the condition that no one will believe her. The Greek gods keep the future to themselves, and human hope (Pandora's box) yields only misery. Only Heraclitus challenges the view of eternal substance with his doctrines of flow and struggle. In the struggle against boundaries, humans exert their freedom and possibility. Yet *logos* wisdom calls flux back to its rhythmic harmony and recalls human energies to human fate.[23]

The boundaries, limitations, and the destiny of all creation are determined by force coming from the highest god. Represented by the Greek goddesses Tyche and Haimarmene, this force constitutes a necessity at once benign and malignant. It is only as this force is imbued with the Christian wisdom of providence; as a loving God, alive in creation in Christ, dismantles demonic fatalism (Romans 8) and assures nature of a benevolent and creative future, that scientific and technical confidence can emerge.

It is the Greek religion that first discerned the divine in nature in terms of order and meaning. This contributes a basis of modern science, as well as the distortion it must discard. The concept of the divine in nature is most nobly expressed not in Greek religion but in philosophy. We must now summarize this aspect of the Greek consciousness with illustrative reference to the philosophy of Plato and the theology of Aristotle. Although Plato's political thought and Aristotle's physics are more relevant to our understandings of nature, the themes chosen highlight the interaction between the technical and the ethical consciousness.

Greek natural science was based on the principle that the world of nature is saturated or permeated by mind.[24] On the one hand, this view provides a confidence in the reliability of and the discernibility of nature (logos unites human reason and nature) that can initiate science. On the other hand, modern consciousness must modify this view. In the Cartesian tradition, the Western mind goes so far as to separate mind from matter, in order to release scientific mentality to its full potential.

What are the central factors in the Greek philosophic consciousness? For Plato, there is an unqualified spiritual substratum that undergirds all matter. The causality which informs reality is intrinsic, in the sense that it is the deliberate working of mind or soul (*nous*). Taking the concepts of Anaximenes and interweaving the thoughts of Parmenides, we have an emphasis on nature being balanced from within. There is no necessity for an external cosmos because *this* cosmos is inherently perfect and complete. Nothing external can destroy it because it is sufficient unto itself. At this point, Plato argues that the available quantity of each of the elements has been used up in the cosmos. Now, through internal dialectics of movement and mixture, they are rearranged but not consumed.

Some of the critical debate in technological planning and assessment today focuses upon a critical point introduced by Plato. If entropy, or the second law of thermodynamics, is true in its emphasis on the "wearing down" or dissociative process in energy, and if there is no fundamental equilibrium in nature on which humans can rely, then we have a very different range of ethical imperatives than would be the case in some "steady state" universe.

Plato makes an important departure from the static Parmenidean concept of nature when he claims that motions are ordered by time. The maker of this world, the timeless Creator, made it one world, a perfect living cosmos, in the process of time. It is created, not unbegotten as in Parmenides. Its coherence and purpose are inherent only in its contingence to the Creator. Knowledge is intrinsically ethical: love and knowledge are essentially related, and proper knowledge discerns the form of the good.[25]

Initially, we must note the importance of the notion that there is a reality that transcends empirical reality. Plato speaks of the ideas which constitute the true essence of things. Beyond all material reality lies a transcendent order which constitutes, arranges, and directs it. Although in later neoplatonism, the philosophy prompted a disregard and denigration of matter, even a denial of nature's reality in some expressions, the early unadulterated concept as we find it in Pythagorus, for example, is an important element in the development of scientific consciousness. Weizsäcker has noted the importance of the Platonic idealism in the development of theoretical physics.[26] The theoretical consciousness from which science and technology emerge is a high-level process of abstraction, possible only through vivid faith in the predictability and order of nature.[27]

Plato's natural philosophy enables us to speak of a wisdom in nature. Nature can speak to us, can remind us of her inherent boundaries and intrinsic possibilities, because nature is a manifestation of the divine. Nature is alive. The world-soul that activates and energizes nature is the same soul that transforms mind. The same movement that produces time in nature affects movement in human consciousness. The cosmology, epistemology, and ethics of the Greeks eventually blend into the Christian worldview that constitutes the Western mind.

In Plato's *Timaeus* as one element of this structure of conscious-ness, we have a theory of the fundamental structures of matter, based on the traditions of Democritus and Empedocles.[28] Plato takes the four traditional elements (fire, water, earth, air) and adds mathematical theory as the rationalizing factor. He debated the skeptical philosophers who insisted that sensory data were the only avenue of knowledge and that therefore we have only "sub-jectivity in values." In Plato, we have the argument that things are permanent and essential, a reliable starting point for human knowledge and happiness.

Plato's natural philosophy was grounded in Pythagorean geo-metry and Eleatic thought. The system undergoes alteration and elaboration in Aristotle and subsequent science. But here we find the origins of the natural philosophy that will develop into mod-ern scientific consciousness.

Aristotle, of course, is a better observer and empiricist than Plato. His science is sufficiently brilliant that fifteen hundred years after its original expression, it so invigorated scientific creativity in the West that the modern scientific world was launched. Through the mediation of Arabic culture, Aristotle's theology, as part of his metaphysics, lies behind his philosophic speculation and deep ethi-cal reflection. It is also the age of the mystery religions. Aristotle shares in all aspects of this world, living and teaching day by day on the Philosopher's Terrace in Athens, where all ideas come under discussion. He comes to understand that the idea of God is required by the heart as well as by the intellect. Theology is the highest of the sciences, because "among existing things one is bet-ter than another; therefore there is a best, which must be the divine." [29] Humans know that the stars and heavens, the beauty of earth and sea are the "mighty works of the gods."

Because there is change, there must be a chain of causality backward and forward that necessitates a cycle of motion. There must therefore be an eternal substance that activates all of reality. This center of all process is itself immaterial and unmoved. The unmoved mover touches what it moves without being touched by it. God is the initial and efficient cause, moving all nature accord-ing to a love that attracts desire in the objects of creation. Aristotle does not affirm God as the creator of the world; rather, matter is ungenerated, eternal. God is the informing principle and activating power of all nature.

For Aristotle, the prime mover is pure form and pure actuality. It is the power that sustains all things—matter, animals and humankind—in their yearning for actualization. This ultimate reality is also the good. In the power with which it draws all nature, the good or purposive in everything is realized.

God does not have a practical interest in the world for Aristotle. In no way is God affected by temporal and material processes.[30] Humans are given active reasoning, which enables them to distinguish between the matter and the potentiality, the necessity and the possibility, and the good and evil of things.[31] Here the affirmation of human responsibility in scientific and technical consciousness is affirmed. Active reason enables humans to take given materials and facilitate the promotion process toward actuality and beauty.

Here, as in Plato, we have a view of nature and human perception of the natural world, where knowledge, technique, and ethics are intertwined. Nature bears intrinsic purposes which humans can discern. Human responsibility is to allow nature her purpose and assist in that action, which is guarded by the goal of love. There is a moral obligation to both human knowledge and its technological tasks.

The theology of Aristotle is ultimately unsatisfactory. Although Averroës ascribed to God the laws of nature, and Thomas Aquinas interpreted God theistically, we have here a naturalistic conception of divinity. Modern science claims that spirit must ultimately be extricated from nature to allow material autonomy and provide free range for human moral action. Aristotle's influence is great, of course, on the emergence of scientific mentality. Most scientists with any philosophic sophistication attribute a great debt to Aristotle. Whitehead ends most of his books with an excursus on neo-Aristotelian theology.[32] Aristotle's work is appreciated by Whitehead and Teilhard de Chardin because of its dispassionate metaphors, one in which the reality of God is affirmed out of the process of nature, without any vested religious or ethical interests.[33]

With Aristotle, Whitehead asks that we conceive "actuality as in essential relation to an unfathomable possibility."[34] Here we see the powerful ethical relevance of his thought to our developing consciousness, which seeks to ethically plan and assess technology. When possibility is viewed in terms of human responsibility in the actualizing process, we have established a framework for relevant ethical action.

In Aristotle, a simultaneously complementary and contradictory notion to Plato's ideas is introduced. In the concept of Telos, God is the highest form, "pure form," form without matter. This is the force that drives everything toward its perfection. Although here again we have a notion that modern science must reject in some of its aspects, it is this concept that gives the idea of directionality and progress in nature. Although Aristotle cannot grasp evolution because of the limitation of his empirical studies and the idea of fixed species, he does introduce the idea of dynamism in nature, which becomes fundamental to modern thought in the life sciences. Because of its vital dynamic, the Aristotelian ethical heritage is especially relevant to judgments that must be made about the concourse of life.

The Stoic influence in the late ancient world cannot be overlooked. The Stoics also noted the principle of movement in nature. The Logos is the force by which humankind was able to take cognizance of nature and develop theoretical and practical reason. The Logos also mediates the moral law at the heart of nature, by which all things consist, move, and have their being. When modern thought speaks of the natural law which grounds humankind's natural moral rights, we recollect a Stoic insight.

Together, these Platonic, Aristotelian, and late Greek elements contribute to build the medieval mind from which scientific consciousness and technology (the Benedictines) emerge. A concept of nature and God, within which nature enjoys an autonomy, a freedom, yet a contingency rendering it predictable and orderly, is the legacy of this tradition.

In conclusion, we note several aspects of the Greek concept of nature that contribute to the building of modern consciousness.

1. The view of providence emerges as nature is mediated from a divine being. Clement of Rome, in singing to the "Great Demiurge," witnessed to the great influence of Plato on early Christian thought. When the world is providentially ordered, humans approach the world with confidence and energetic creativity, rather than with foreboding and withdrawal.
2. In Greek thought, nature is transparent. The divine shines though all nature. Greek "Icons" reveal this element of Eastern consciousness. When nature loses this transparency, it is dedivinized, and "things become merely objects of technical activity."[35] At this point, the modern scientific consciousness of humankind is in need of reawakening.

We still live in the infancy of scientific mentality. This is a period when we are enamored of the fruits of empirical method. We make positivistic analysis normative and object to any mention of the dimension of spirit or transcendence. We refuse to allow mystery or transcendence to distort our perception. Mircea Eliade has noted that primitive humans possessed a grace lacking in moderns. Primitive humans worshiped the sacred revealed through objects, rather than the objects themselves, while for us it is still an either/or proposition. We need to rediscover that it is transcendence which undergirds our scientific mentality. In our time, Weizsäcker, Heisenberg, and others affirm this "otherness" as necessary to good ethics and good science.[36] The Greeks corroborate our thesis about ethics that "ought" is embedded in "is." Though natural law has fallen upon hard times in our positivistic postmodern age, humanity's heightened sympathy with natural process gives this epistemology and ethics more currency.

Finally, the idea that there is an "order to nature" (Whitehead), or a cosmic harmony, is fundamental to Greek cosmology. "*O Theos aei geometrei*" (God acts as a geometrician) goes the adage. Tillich notes that Augustine abandons the theological ideas of Manicheanism through his study of astronomy.[37] The legacy of Greek-European history is the notion of cosmic order, rooted in Pythagorean mathematics and Greek philosophic wisdom, gathered in the insight of Plato and Aristotle. Here the foundations of a Christian philosophy of reality and the modern mind are formed, and here, together with the added influences of Roman order, lie the foundations of Christian civilization.

The Apocalyptic Expectation of Crisis in Nature and History

Interposed between the end of classical culture and the emergence of Christian civilization lies another historical development that profoundly effects the intellectual, technical, and ethical consciousness of the human race. What we might call an apocalyptic mentality strongly asserts itself in the ancient world of both old-oriental and Semitic Theocracy and ontocracy. Greek rationality now begins to crumble and yield to a new synthetic Christian civilization and consciousness. The mood of crisis and expectancy emerges, reaches a high pitch in Judaism around 200 B.C.E. (the period of Daniel in biblical history), and climaxes around 100 A.D. during the period of Roman governance. The mentality is important to our thesis because it creates a deep impression in the emerging human consciousness and retains a lingering significance to the present day. When a thousand teenagers fly to India to sit at the feet of the maharaja, when an M.I.T. group announces impending global catastrophe, when Robespierre sings the dawning of the world's first republic, when Thomas Munzer flames revolutionary fervor, when Montanus proclaims himself "Father, Son, and Paraclete," when the disaffected are ambushed at Ruby Ridge or firebombed at Waco, or when they in turn incinerate Oklahoma City, or as unibombers, plant missiles at Northwestern, we witness the surfacing of this highly ambivalent element in our consciousness.

The apocalyptic imagination captures human devotion when crisis is impending in nature and history. It appears in what Toynbee calls "times of trouble." Generally, it is precipitated by the wasting of a once-stable political order or a once-satisfying worldview. To trace the development of this consciousness and analyze its character is the purpose of this section.

Although apocalyptic awareness is found among many peoples down through history, it is awakened with great intensity among the Hebrews. Although the mentality can be found in Greek or other peoples who have cyclic concepts of nature and time, the doctrine of a universal conflagration (*ekpurosis*), which sweeps the world back into Zeus, is a recurring event that lacks finality. It remains for the cosmic notion of natural seasons and times to be historicized in Judaism, then given a progressive linear orientation, to provide the basis for genuine apocalypticism. Apocalyptic is the way the disruption and incompleteness of nature and history imprints human consciousness, and the way that sheer divine power imprints contingency on the human spirit. It is also the mode of thought by which anxiety and dread in the human spirit is projected upon reality.

History in this view moves rapidly to the conclusion of the world year, where it collapses and makes ready for the birth of the new age. Restitution (*apocatastasis*) of all things, including the freshness of creation, is assured as the old age passes. In Hebrew apocalyptic, the two aeons are opposed to each other as the new ruptures history by its appearance. The apocalyptic element is introduced into a sense of reality with the concepts of time and history. The coming aeon evokes all the expectancy and revolutionary passion in the human spirit. From the pathos of the Babylonian exile onward, we find ingrained in Hebrew consciousness that blending of despair and hope, that longing for redemption, within which all worldly attempts at order and government are seen as futile, and catastrophe is seen as hope because it provides the ruins on which God's kingdom can then be built.

The scheme in Daniel, for example, becomes the basis of all later apocalyptic chronologies. The statue that Nebuchadnezzar sees (Daniel 2) allegorizes the successive eras of history as nations move toward judgment. The metallic age chronology is used. The head is golden, the body silver, the hips bronze, and the feet iron and clay. Specifically, the historical kingdoms are portrayed by the four beasts (Daniel 7). From the succession of Babylonian, Medes, Persian, and Greek kingdoms will arise the "Harsh King" in the last days.

In this mentality, the crisis or judgment is not an historical or natural event, but a supernatural one, evidenced in cosmic catastrophe, epiphenomenal to time and space. From the turmoil of the last hours emerge the powers of Antichrist and Messiah. The dragon representing primeval chaos again arises, and the great cataclysm begins. In the end, the eternal kingdom of God will be established. "It shall crush all these kingdoms and bring them to an end, and it shall stand forever" (Daniel 2:44*b* NRSV).

Apocalyptic mentality is transformed into several types of expectation of God's kingdom in the Christian community. These will be thoroughly discussed when we survey the contribution of Christian eschatology to our theme. The principal legacy we must note at this point concerns the Apocalypse of the New Testament.

In the book of Revelation, a new concept of millennialism is injected into Western consciousness. Although not strictly apocalyptic, it differs from essential Jewish and Christian eschatology. The literal faith in the idea is not nearly as important as the broad implication. At the end of "this evil age" an angel from heaven will come, chain the dragon, "the ancient serpent who is the Devil and Satan," and cast him into the bottomless pit, there to be sealed for a thousand years. Then the martyr and faithful shall be resuscitated to reign with Christ for the millennium, after which the dead will be raised, last judgment will come, and the new heaven and earth will be fashioned (Revelation 20ff.). This promise, as Ernst Benz remarks, has had a revolutionary effect on history.[38]

The millennial idea transforms consciousness in a way that Jewish apocalyptic could not, because of the way "it gives concrete ideas to hope and imagination."[39] Jewish apocalyptic spoke of an otherworldly, radically discontinuous kingdom. In the early church and in numerous subsequent sacred and secular expressions, the millennial hope has given rise to concrete expectation of and commitment to political, technological, and natural utopia. This hope expects the restitution of all things, in the sense of the coming of a golden age or paradise. In the Puritan millennium, for example, of the seventeenth century, science and medicine will discover the secrets of life, universal education will come to be, infant mortality will cease, and smallpox will be banished.

Apocalyptic consciousness prompts both an attitude and a

propensity to action. Here is the point of relevance to ethics and technology. The attitude, to use the rubrics of Benz, is one of prayer, prophecy and progress.

The prayer of the Christian, raptured in apocalyptic ecstasy, is "Come, Lord!" This prayer and fervent plea can be also for the end of the world. The ancient Didache, a report on the teaching of the earliest Christian community, records this prayer: "Let grace come and let this world pass away. Hosanna to the God of David." [40] The longing for the kingdom of God is accompanied by the passion that this world, full of terror and tragedy, will come to a quick end.

Although the attitude engendered by this expectancy is not always technological activity, it is not "just waiting," as we might expect. Sometimes it has been accompanied by a lust for destruction (*après moi, le déluge*). More often, it has fostered a careful activity of preparation, orderliness, and a high sense of responsibility. In the Puritan legacy of Christian apocalyptic, for example, we have the passion to do one's best in the world, for the time being. The attitude, however, in its radically apocalyptic expressions, certainly does not contribute to the building of the earth. The veil of this present reality will be torn back, and the new reality, the creation of God, not humankind, will be disclosed. Mystery, myth, mysticism—all derive from the Greek word *musterion*, to close the eyes or mouth. The open is closed, the dark and hidden are brought to light. Sometimes, it is clear, this attitude has fostered a positively destructive technical action to hasten the long-awaited apocalypse. Not only the specific modern technological horrors such as the Nazi state, but perhaps the extremes of the revolutionary history of the last two centuries that seek to rush in the Kingdom by human effort can be viewed in this light. [41]

To conclude this point, I might recount the personal experience of speaking on a platform with brain physiologist José Delgado, in a southern American city. As we discussed the prospects of a future where conditioning and electrochemical manipulation of the brain would be routine, we noticed a decided apathy on the part of the audience. We felt they had neither terror nor excitement over these prospects. We queried them with a specific question: "For how many here is it an ultimate value that the world and the human race continue after your death?" Twenty percent of the audience raised their hands. Only a small percentage could affirm that long-range survival value. To us, this was sure indication of the validity of Maslow's frightening priority list of human needs. In this enumeration, needs of self-gratification are preeminent. Concern for others and for the future is way down the list.

The second attitude engendered by millennialism concerns prophesy. Benz notes that apocalyptic vision "leaps over the present and anticipates the future." [42] When a person or group long and pray enough for a particular future, it either comes, through self-fulfilling prophecy, or they believe that it comes. One senses the evident contribution of this mentality to technological planning, as well as ethical assessment of technology. If we prepare for a certain future and bank our hopes upon it, it probably will come to pass.

Concern for justice and righteousness accompanies the prophetic apocalyptic consciousness. Crisis, in the biblical sense, is always judgment or separation. Judgment arrives by reason of human injustice. The future has a foreboding quality because the righteousness of God draws a cleavage that divides good and evil. It is clear that the heart of apocalyptic mentality responds to this awareness. Indeed, the enduring practical relevance of the consciousness responds to the moral law that resides at the heart of nature and history.

Finally, the idea of millennium injects a spirit of progress into history. Transformed into the nonapocalyptic theology of John's Gospel, for example, we deal with the idea that the kingdom of God is gradually unfolding in history, as the Age of the Holy Spirit works creatively through and among people. The idea that we are able, through our efforts, to pursue utopia or millennium and that we therefore are responsible for that action is a great technical and ethical impetus. Although we have here a mentality that expresses a gentle eschatology rather than a violent apocalypticism, the roots of the former reside in the latter.

Perhaps the principal gift of apocalyptic consciousness within human experience is the knowledge that all things are contingent, not only upon some substratum of support, but upon the future.

Pannenberg has clarified this contingency in his essay with Klaus Muller.[43] In this essay, he argues that not only is reliable perception of nature contingent upon faith (Einstein), but the necessity of contingency is fundamental to natural process itself. This contingency is not meaningless or directionless, but is contingent upon the "power of the future," which is God.

Stated somewhat poetically, the scientific import of apocalyptic consciousness would say, with G. K. Chesterton, that God commands every morning the sun to rise and every evening the moon to sleep. Heidegger would write, "Contemporary man anticipates the unknowable of the present age not through his powerful transformations of the world but at best waiting for the appearance of God" (my translation).[44] The faith here expressed is that beyond our clearest designs and most careful planning lies the unknown, the unexpected. The element of consciousness, apocalyptic yet pregnant with responsibility, is captured in a conversation of the young physicist Weizsäcker with Karl Barth. Visiting him at Basel at the time of the creation of the first nuclear weapons, he asked Barth if one should continue in science, given the terrifying possibilities and consequences. Barth answered simply, "If you believe what Christians always have said they believe, that Christ is coming again, you may continue."

The enduring relevance and ethical import of apocalyptic consciousness is like that enigmatic counsel to the young physicist. If God is in control of history, God will bring it to its consummate purpose. We may have difficulty with the obscure symbolism of the mentality. We may have a secular understanding by which we expect the cosmos to slowly dissipate its energies into oblivion. We may expect a global holocaust of our own doing, such as a nuclear disaster. If we believe, however, that this is God's world, we must, with Rowley, "find some way of translating the faith of the apocalypticists that . . . the divine purpose will be achieved." [45]

The Christian Hope for the Future

We have argued thus far that a certain worldview has made us the people we are and has created the technical enterprise, including that of medicine and health care. Within this worldview, we find a commensurate ethic, sufficient to guide those constituent projects. In the apocalyptic consciousness of late Judaism and early Christianity, the element of time gradually disappears as a quality of the future. Waiting becomes increasingly frustrating, and the farsighted expectation of the consummation of history becomes less acceptable. The future rushes forward and upward, and eventually loses its temporality, becoming localized as a transcendent moment. The "little apocalypse" in Mark 13 and parallels speaks of impending natural and historical crises (earthquakes, famines, wars), but translates it into the hour which neither humans nor angels, not even the Son, can know (Mark 13:32). Here, as in other moments of historical crisis, hope consciously transforms its expectation into radically external or existential nontemporal forms. The world now waits for one who will bring the hope of heaven down to earth.

It is in these "times of troubles" that Jesus comes into Galilee, preaching the arrival of the kingdom. His words and actions attest to a new power present among people. His followers fashion a community of hope, informed not only by apocalyptic expectation,[46] but by an eschatological awareness that is to fundamentally alter history. It is to this building block in the structure of our ethical and technical consciousness that we now turn. In the idea of the kingdom of God, we have the blending of hope, ethics, of energies and expectations that will be released into the technical sphere of human life. Although much has been written to describe the eschatological soil from which technology emerges,[47] the analysis of consciousness formative of both technical and ethical reason needs further elaboration and specification to our purpose.

Although one can convincingly argue that modern culture is completely secularized and that contemporary scientific mentality possesses no theological dimension, I will argue, in the tradition of Whitehead and Carl Friedrich von Weizsäcker, that historically, subliminally, and residually, our technological mentality and ethical sensitivity emerge from this composite religio-philosophical tradition. The purpose of this argument is to establish this continuity and to locate the link between technical and ethical awareness, so as to relate how we should act in accordance with the way we think. The thesis may be stated more sharply by a warning. If we fail to ascertain the causal roots of our activities and responsibly perpetuate those values that have made us what we are and prompted us to do what we are doing, we stand in danger of destroying ourselves by our own creative activity.

I wish to argue for a contemporary ethic, which although rooted in tradition, is not nostalgic reminiscence of former times, nor an absolutization of previous insight, but is value-directed toward the future. In an important sense, the ethical legacy of Christian eschatology claims our responsibility exactly within radically new, unprecedented, and completely ambiguous situations. We are called today to solve problems that never before have arisen. Although, as we hope to show, traditional wisdom can help us negotiate our dilemmas, we must be aware of the profound implication of Parousic faith: the past does not have the answer.

We will look first at the beginnings of Christian eschatology by discerning the nature of the Kingdom in Jesus and Paul, and the formation of the New Testament consciousness. Second, we will follow the understanding of eschatological development. Following a brief section on revolution and technology, we will examine the divergence and convergence of modern scientific thought to and from this history, and see how this constitutes modern consciousness.

When we begin with Jesus' preaching of the kingdom of God or his self-consciousness, we approach some of the most difficult areas of New Testament research.[48] Controversy lingers as to whether the idea of "Kingdom" has spatial-temporal or only existential meaning. Perrin points to two converging traditions that can be discerned in Jesus' teaching. The Greek concept (*basileia tou theou*) regularly connotes both space and time. The Aramaic *Malkuth shamayim*, with its old Hebrew equivalents, connotes the reign of God, God's kingly rule. Both nations are secular and historical. Bultmann and others demythologize Kingdom language and find its referent in existential experience. Although the debate is intriguing, it is the dual emphasis that is important for our thesis. To exclusively emphasize one understanding is to distort the fullness of the New Testament witness.

The same must be said for the long debate on the nature of the Kingdom's actualization. (While the decision as to whether the Kingdom is "realized" [Dodd] or futuristic [Schweitzer] is absolutely critical for theology, in our thesis, the reality of the Kingdom in human consciousness is pivotal.) In a total perspective of reality, Jesus proclaims God's claim on space, time, and existence. This radical claim is proffered to each individual person and to collective humanity bound in nations. God's kingdom now ruptures human life at that point where being and time coincide in the yet nonactualized future. As contemporary historical scholarship shows, the essence of Jesus' life and teaching involves justice, confrontation of evil, and helping love for people in need. We find here a decisive moment in the history of human well-being.[49]

For Jesus, God is drawing near to God's creation, to work God's will with urgently compelling power. This coming is accompanied by signs, wonders, and miracles. All nature knows that it is caught up with a new urgency in a qualitatively new reality (Matthew 13:31 ff.). Gustav Dalman, who early in this century spelled out the meaning of the fact that Jesus was a Jew who thought and spoke Aramaic, claims that for Jesus, "the sovereignty of God meant the divine power which from the present onwards with continuous progress, effectuates the renovation of the world." [50] Despite the obvious influence of Ritschl, we note here the cosmic dimension of Jesus' understanding of Kingdom. When we review the history of theology as it interprets eschatology, we find a continuing dialectic between the cosmic and existential interpretations that indicate the union in Jesus' self-consciousness. This would prompt us to hold the two emphases in tension.

The ethical import of this point was stressed by Joseph Sittler in an address to the World Council of Churches. Unless God's Kingdom encompasses both existence and world, it is not comprehensive and all-consuming. Something remains external to God's sovereignty. "The actual human existence will be tempted to reduce the redemption of humankind to what purgation, transformation, forgiveness, and blessedness is available by an 'angelic' escape from the cosmos of natural and historical fact." [51] Only a cosmic consciousness of the Kingdom and a cosmic setting for eschatology can do justice to the life and teachings of Jesus and provide the basis for technical responsibility.[52]

In addition to the cosmic dimension of Jesus' announcement and embodiment of the Kingdom, eschatology, as rooted in his life and teaching, has an ethical dimension. Immediately when Jesus emerges from the wilderness to preach in Galilee, he proclaims, "The time is fulfilled, and the kingdom of God is at hand; repent, and believe in the gospel" (Mark 1:15 RSV). The impending crisis of Kingdom come is not a comforting assurance. It provokes earth-shaking and life-changing response.

Throughout the Gospels, the intent of Jesus' preaching, miracles, and healing is not to impress people, but to glorify God, restore shalom and wholeness, and therein save persons and the world. The apostolic band moves out from Jerusalem to the corners of the empire, in response to this expectation of saving renewal of life in its righteousness. When churches fall into idleness while waiting for the parousia, they are reminded that expectation requires active response, not discouraged waiting (see 1 Thessalonians, 5). We shall note that the emergence of eschatological consciousness into the modern world is also accompanied by the same emphasis on response.

The final point to be made concerning the Kingdom in Jesus is the element of healing. One of the things I cannot understand regarding New Testament interpretation is the disparity between the emphasis on healing in Jesus' ministry and the attention given to it in scholarship. The Gospels mark the coming of the Kingdom step by step, with signs and healings. Although the liberation of modern medicine from demonology can explain the scientific inability to understand these events, this factor cannot rationalize the theological reluctance to discern their meaning. Jesus comes to make sick people well. He heals and mends broken bodies. This indeed is evidence of the Kingdom's presence (Luke 7:18-23). "Have you brought God's Kingdom?" asks the imprisoned John the Baptist. "What do you see and hear? The blind see, the lame walk, the lepers are cleansed, the deaf hear, and the dead are raised, the poor now hear the good news." Jesus releases imprisoned minds. He saves and heals. *Salvation* and *healing* are the same word in Greek (*soteria*). *Sickness*, in its profound sense, and *sin* are the same (Luther: *curvatur en se* = bent in on self)—obsession with past, with nonlife, with self—self-obsession to the exclusion of the other, the world, and God.

The kingdom comes from within persons as it comes to persons. It comes from hidden depths of the earth as it comes down to earth. The essence of the awareness is that new reality brings wholeness and wholesomeness. The Kingdom ushers in ethical power (the good) because it releases human life and nature from the demonic (evil). Such a simple point, so neglected in our understanding of what God releases into human history, is fundamental to subsequent ethical and technical consciousness. The minute we grasp this point, we understand the growing aversion to destruction and disease, and the powerful yearning for peace and healing that characterizes our hope today. The focus of this book, the ethical quest for life and health, is firmly anchored in the quality of eschatological hope. The grand hope for health and life, the goal of medicine, is concurrent with underlying spiritual expectation.

When I hope for healing, it is a quest of soul, mind, and body. I may die and yet be healed. Human hope is a quest into which is gathered all existence and environment. Being saved while the earth is destroyed would have no meaning. All time and nature that constitute my personality are captured in the hope for salvation that is evoked by Christ and his Kingdom. When I stand with someone fractured in body, mind, or soul, I do not stand apart, for Christ's reality is my reality. When a bomb explodes and kills a child, my life is drawn toward hell; for the child and I share the same cosmos, the same history, the same flesh. When in love I meet another, all nature participates, for love endures all things. God is love. There is crisis in God's coming (John 9:39). Jesus' kingdom leads him to the cross, where his crown is of thorns. In the coming of the Kingdom, God's gift and our task, deep cosmic pain is the mark of progress and growth. All nature and history resemble nothing so much, says Teilhard de Chardin, as the way of a cross. Cosmic scope, ethical demand, healing and pain, are the qualities of the kingdom of God in the preaching of Jesus.

For secular and scientific-minded readers, let me venture a comment to relate this strange distant world of Jesus' life and consciousness to ours. Certainly we no longer perceive reality in monarchic fashion. It is hard, despite Walt Disney's efforts, for us to think of kingdoms. Like Laplace, we find no need for an external god hypothesis in our day-to-day empirical work. Yet I would venture that the reality of what Jesus spoke of as Kingdom is vivid today to anyone who is really alive. Anyone who knows the thrill of discovery; anyone who feels the mystery of healing; anyone who senses the energy of human communication; anyone who hopes without illusion; anyone who knows moral outrage perceives the proleptic and is experiencing the ethical and liberating quality of the Kingdom.

At this point we must consider the contribution of the apostle Paul to Christian eschatological awareness. The Pauline eschatology, focusing on the new human being, the new humanity and new creation (2 Corinthians 5:17) has had a determinative effect on subsequent thought. For Paul, humans exist in a constant struggle to affirm freedom and possibility (Spirit) or bondage (flesh). All events bring to humans the call and confrontation of God. We must continually choose to love or not to love, to be or not to be. The struggle is one of choosing to become what one could become, or to choose the past. When humans wish to remain as they are, they choose sin; they deny Jesus. Ebeling has called Jesus the "future opening word." When humans are confronted with this future, this possibility, this demand, they are confronted with the kingdom of God. Biblically understood, the kingdom of God expresses its demand by pulling humanity into time and history, which is into responsibility.

For Paul, the fullness of time has come historically (Galatians 4:4) and existentially (Galatians 2:15-16) as God sends Jesus into the world. The apocalypse has been fulfilled. Eternal life has appeared. The end time for humanity has come. Just as in the cross of Christ one died for all, therefore all have died. In the atonement, one has obeyed, therefore all are justified (Romans 5). Humans are set free from the law and released to life, which is possibility. So too the creation is being released from its bondage into the glorious liberty of the children of God (Romans 8).

For Paul, intrinsic anthropology is the essence of eschatology. Although nature too groans in the travail of freedom toward redemption (Romans 8), it is caught up together in the new creature being fashioned in Christ, the new Adam (Ephesians 1:20ff.; Colossians 1:15ff.). Humanity is the nexus or bearer of the new creation, of the Kingdom. "To be human," says Harvey Cox, "is to be on the way to something else. . . . The human is the hoper, his basic stance is that of creative expectation, a hope that engenders action in the present to shape the future." [53] Bloch, of course, has located human uniqueness in his expectation and striving for the Kingdom. Unlike Paul, the emphasis here is on temporal hope.

In Paul, the basic historic/ahistoric cleavage that is to mark all subsequent Christian hope is present. Although for Paul humans are released to genuine historical freedom in the existence Christ offers, it is an existence within which the dialectics of sin and grace interplay in continual ontic tension. Paul seeks to explain the fact that Christians may be called to wait long generations for the consummation, maintaining all the while an urgent expectation. Bultmann has shown how "the Pauline conception of historicity and his unfolding of the dialectic of Christian existence contains the solution of the problem of history and eschatology as it was raised by the delay of the parousia of Christ." [54] Christian hope is about some new thing happening to the body, death's power being obviated, new creation emerging. The implications for life and health are obvious.

The influence of Paul's attempt to existentialize eschatology is unfolded in Augustine and the subsequent "two kingdoms" doctrine. This dichotomy creates the modern cleavage between "spiritual" and "technical" realms. Augustine combines Pauline anthropology with a Platonic ontology that pictures God and the good as eternal forms, neither unaffected by nor affecting the movement of history. This combination of Hellenistic and biblical views accounts for the compromise in Augustinian ethics. The good is to be found only in that ever-transcendent moment which we can grasp in faith. This results in a dualism and pessimism which disparages matter and the secular; it seeks the comfort of some "two kingdoms" view of reality and fosters pietism and

escape from worldly responsibility. "If God is no longer understood as coming into this world but as a being different from the
world who is the goal of pious longing, then a tendency to escape
the world is rooted in the very idea of God."[55]

The effect of the ahistorical is felt in many tragedies of the
modern world. "The history of this world is a bad dream to the
monk on Mount Athos. . . . Christianity had always preached a
complete indifference toward history."[56] In reflecting on Russian
history, Rosenstock-Huessy discerns that *Geist* of Eastern Chris-
tendom, where spirit and matter are so close, yet ever distinct, so
that spirit shines through matter as divine oversight radiates
through the eyes of the icons.

Ever since the time of the early church, Christians have questioned whether they really belong in space and time, and whether
God's purpose has to do with this world. This mentality is heightened in historical crisis. "Blessed is our generation," states the
apocryphal Acts of Andrew. "We are not thrown down, for we have
been recognized by the light. We do not belong to time, which
would dissolve us. We are not a product of motion, which would
destroy us again. We belong to the greatness toward which we are
striving."[57] An examination of primitive Christianity clearly
emphasizes, however, that God works God's purposes in time and
space and that Christians' responsibility resides in this world. In
the divine plan of salvation, God's *kairoi* (moments of time) occur
in *chronos* in the arena of aeon (space of time). Christian time is linear. It moves in the direction of consummation (*pleroma*). It is the
compromise of this linear notion of time to metaphysics, according
to Oscar Cullmann, that blurs the vision of biblical eschatology.[58]

The ahistoricism, though deeply affected by Paul's theology, yet
distorting biblical eschatology in subsequent interpretations, does
not reduce the power of Paul's eschatological vision. For the
Christian, history is the arena where the drama of redemption
occurs. Nature is the fellow creature, yearning for redemption
together with humanity in Christ. Our action with self, with
others, or with nature reflects the ambivalence of sin and the
good, and thus bears responsibility. Sin, in the Pauline anthropology and cosmology, makes its claim on events. Yet grace, that

coming of God which meets our hope, urges creation toward redemption. As Johannes Metz states it:

> Sin has something violent about it. It forces on the world something other than its own worldly being. Sin does not tolerate and let things be themselves. . . . It overpaints, distorts, forces, destroys things. But grace is freedom, it bestows upon things the scarcely measured depths of their own being. It calls the world into its perfect worldliness, *Gratia perficit naturam.*[59]

From the apostolic age until the period when Christianity is consolidated into the Roman Empire, we witness a theological struggle to maintain the vigor of eschatological expectation. The Kingdom does not come as expected. In the second century, Tertullian and the Montanists attempt to spiritually reinvigorate the church with awakened expectation of the end. Seeing in their own revival a breath of the Spirit, they lay claim to special blessing and vision, and thus began the long parade of sectarian revolutionary movements that make a significant contribution to Western consciousness. Tillich remarks that the Montanist movement evidences the prophetic poverty of the "establishing" church and the growing neglect of eschatology.[60] The power and presence of God are now mediated through the sacramental ministrations of the church. In Origen, we have the first great synthesis of Greek natural wisdom and Christian revelation. In his logos theology, we find emphasis given to the sweeping magnitude of redemption. In his doctrine of the restitution of all things, we find an emphasis on spiritualized eschatology. The second coming of Christ is enacted in the souls of believers.[61] This element becomes the medieval legacy.

The medieval world can be interpreted as a massive cultural search for the kingdom of God, expressed as a yearning and soaring reach toward its perfection.[62] Chesterton has called the Gothic cathedrals "a thousand arrows shot toward heaven." We note a significant departure from primitive Christian expectation of the future. Here the mentality is not so much a passive waiting but an active pursuit of the Kingdom. The Ravenna mosaics, the brilliant theological system of Thomas Aquinas and the rose window at

Chartres can be explained only in terms of this beautiful attitude of faith, not so much expectant as expressive and jubilant.

In medieval thought, we have a blending of hope with ethical and technical consciousness. Strangely enough, a critical period is that of the spiritual mystics. The visionary monk Joachim of Floris predicted, in a book on the Apocalypse, that a new phase of time was beginning on earth. The age of the Old and New Testaments, the Father and the Son, was now yielding to the Age of the Third Testament, the Age of the Spirit. The rigid ecclesiastical structure would now give way to free human creativity and the gentle ethics of Saint Francis. Persons of the spirit would now lead the earth progressively toward its fulfillment. "Joachim," says Benz, "is the first theologian of history who introduced the idea of progress into the theology of history." [63] The spiritualist movement was to have a profound effect upon history. Many of the forerunners of modern science (William of Occam, Nicholas of Cusa, Robert Grosseteste) were influenced by this movement.[64] This critical spirit paved the way for Reformation and Renaissance within which the modern secular consciousness was born.

The Benedictines witness to the unification of religious fervor and technical skill. A joining of the worlds of science and action, of prayer and work, becomes the genius of this movement. The scientific spirit focused in the quest for knowledge is here united with intense practical interests; agricultural activity, watermills, windmills, and canals, along with careful farming, more than tripled the agricultural output of Europe in the tenth century. "It is one of the most amazing facts of Western cultural history," says Benz, "that the striking acceleration and intensification of technological development in post-Carolingian Europe emanated from contemplative monasticism, such as the order of the Benedictines and its later reform orders, the Cluniacs and the Cistercians." [65] For the Benedictines, knowledge of nature evokes responsive care and utilization from humanity.

To illustrate the way these epochs of consciousness we are characterizing are perennial manifestations of the human soul, let us note a current event. In Evanston, where I write, the home of Northwestern University, the first incident of the now famous "unabomber" occurred. Distressed at the intrusion of technology into what his romantic philosophy calls pure nature and free human community, the bomber sends or plants letters or package bombs in laboratories and other technological facilities, or to renowned scientists. To date, three persons have been killed and scores injured. In a 100,000-word statement of his worldview, the modern Luddite claims that overriding technological organization is despoiling and (like his own work) destroying the world and its people. Whenever hope and ambition, even as benign as the Benedictine monastics, turns overly to manipulation, an underlying apocalyptic reaction surfaces.

The technical achievements of the Middle Ages, though impressive, are not as decisive for history as the emerging mentality. Whitehead remarks that this period formed one long training process of the intellect of western Europe, in the sense of order. Even though a sense of historical and social crisis came to grip the late medieval mind, the clear Aristotelian logic and scholastic theology formed the notions of regularity and predictability in the emerging scientific intellect (i.e., Galileo). "The greatest contribution of medievalism to the formation of the scientific movement," writes Whitehead, "is the inexpugnable belief that every detailed occurrence can be correlated with its antecedents in a perfectly defined matter, exemplifying general principles. Without this belief, the incredible labors of scientists would be without hope." [66]

The medieval synthesis eventually had to yield to the modern world. The notions of eternal substance and Aristotelian teleology came under fundamental criticism. Many streams converged to create a new river of philosophical thought. We have mentioned the mystical strain. This tradition with Meister Eckehart, Nicholas of Cusa, and others, constituted a critical mentality which eventually unleashed the modern inquisitive spirit. Mysticism and mathematics were cognate intelligences. There was also a revival of natural philosophy. The thought of Paracelsus, the heights of Arabian and European medicine, and the beginnings of modern chemistry—all attest to a renewed interest in the nature of reality. Finally the great upsurge of empirical research commenced at the dawn of the Renaissance. Foundations for the work of Copernicus,

Kepler, Galileo, and the grand sequence of pioneers of the modern scientific consciousness are laid in the high Middle Ages.

Undergirding the medieval consciousness was an intense faith amplified by fear. Both impulses—to achieve good and avoid evil—feed into the technical and medical project. The orders of society, the processes of nature, the drama of life and death, were patterns in the divine schema. This earth, the human soul, and the holy catholic church are the focus of all the judgmental and gracious energy of Almighty God. Over all reality, and at its end, stands the justice of God. *Dies Irae*, the day of wrath and judgment, determines the eternal destiny of humankind and the earth. Eschatology, though lacking the temporal urgency it had in primitive Christianity, became subsumed in a total wholistic worldview. Strasbourg and the other medieval cathedrals, as well as the frescoes and painting, reflect the influence of Apocalypse, the impending judgment of the earth. Christ, "the lamb slain," becomes the eschatological symbol. Grünewald's moving *Crucifixion* (c. 1490) now at Colmar, France, depicts in Jesus' diseased and wounded body God's absorption and forgiveness of the sin of the world, identification with the sick and wounded, and healing for humanity.

It is not until high Gothic art that we have the beginnings of an eschatological consciousness. There terror and trembling are still evoked before the awesome presence of God, but ecstasy and creative energy are called forth as well. Chartres Cathedral, for example, in its *Last Judgment*, portrays the Christ of the central Tympanum as "a new Savior, no longer the threatening avenger of monastic last judgments, but a mediator between God and humankind."[67]

In the work of Albrecht Dürer, we have the new theological emphasis that is to mark the thought of not only Luther, Buber, and Calvin but of Erasmus and the finest minds of the Catholic reformation. The Renaissance is a time when faith in human creative power is seen to be a correlate of faith in God. The reality of the eschatological future bearing judgment and hope prompts humanity to join God in cooperative redemptive action. Calvin articulates this massive transition in Christian mentality:

> We should not hesitate to expect the advent of the Lord, not
> merely by wishing, but with signs and groans as a most auspicious
> event. For Christ will come to us as a redeemer.[68]

For Calvin, the judgment of God is salvation. The fact that
humans live under judgment means that they live responsibly.
Persons are accountable to their Maker for their actions. Yet
God's justice is not a crushing rejection of all human effort, but
rather a stimulus to high responsibility. The idea of responsibility
to God is precisely the point where Renaissance anthropology
meets the idea of judgment.[69]

Max Weber has shown the way Calvinism contributes to the
Puritan mentality and the resultant history of capitalism. It is not
only fear of judgment that constitutes human motivation, but a
genuine confidence that when one does one's best in the world,
when one *capitalizes* on each moment, when one energetically
derives the fullest significance from each possibility, one cooperates with God in the process of making the world. When the
future is seen as judgment, industry is prompted. It is important
to discern this element beneath the complex of social and economic factors giving rise to modern technology. Progress/devel-
opment is seen not solely as a good or an end in itself, but as an
instrument to pursue human perfection, as either ameliorating
guilt or achieving righteousness.

In the seventeenth century, we see the results of new religious and
scientific worldviews struggling to coexist. Newton weaves theology
into his philosophy of nature under some restraint, as does Laplace.
In the same way, scholastic theology takes over scientific and mathematical methodology. Descartes' philosophy emphasizes mathematical, rational order. It also draws the distinction between mind and
matter. This consciousness enabled science to proceed with a thor-
oughgoing materialistic interpretation of physical nature. At the same
time, theological thought on both wings of the Reformation was satisfied with internally consistent logic and self-contained systems. On
both sides, Protestant and Catholic orthodoxy developed in Europe.
The result was to be expected: A complete "value free" connotation
was placed in scientific work, and theology was stripped of its eschatological power.

Nature in the Cartesian-Newtonian worldview is pictured as a machine with neither spontaneity nor teleology. Science now has to deal with "hard data." Particulate matter, activated by natural laws in a mechanical universe, constitutes the object of scientific inquiry. There may well be a divine Creator, but that force is "out there" and does not intervene in the processes of nature or history. From the theological side, reality also becomes a static system. History is deemphasized, as is the cosmic dimension of New Testament eschatology. Humanity is now part of a highly ordered, highly rational cosmos, the patterns and laws of which are immutable. God, who has defined reality, is now defined by that reality. Extensive scholastic systems of theology are articulated, wherein God's revelation and humankind's knowledge meet in highly rationalistic schemes. In natural theology, immortality of the soul, the logical consequence of human reason, replaces biblical hope in the resurrection. "A spiritualized and individualized eschatology displaced the cosmic and realistic soteriology and Christology of the New Testament." [70]

We have here a return to the Greek cosmic theology. Knowledge of the truth carries with it natural immortality and intuitive morality. Obedience to the codified ethic of necessity engenders righteousness. In the same way that Ignatius called the Lord's Supper the remedy against death, Reformation orthodoxy accepts a pseudo-Platonic rationalism in place of biblical wisdom. [71]

As the Enlightenment glories in human progress, so the eschatological ethic of the Bible is subsumed as a correlate of human reason. "Kant interprets the whole history of Christianity as a gradual advance from a religion of revelation to a religion of reason, by which the Kingdom of God is realized as an ethical state on earth." [72] Religion has nothing to do with nature, but only with the interior life of humans, piety, and ethics. The moral will now synthesizes moral law and freedom within the structures of reason. In a post-Kantian and postmodern world, humans are free to shape technical reality decisively.

The effect of this change of consciousness is, needless to say, revolutionary. The future, formerly seen as coming from the hand of God, becomes a result of human achievement. We witness, in the eighteenth and nineteenth centuries, a period in which the idea of progress is absolutized—fired by a revolutionary consciousness on which we will later comment. We witness the "transition from a religious eschatology that had prevailed almost undisputedly for nearly twenty centuries to a new, soon all-prevailing pseudo-religious eschatology. The Land of Promise and the future final fulfillment were transposed to earth again and into the historical course of time . . . with a revolutionary change of spirit." [73]

At the beginning of the nineteenth century, Condorcet claims that history is completely secularized. The Christian faith, interpreted in the manner of Comte, was only a passing state of superstition, now succeeded by enlightenment, as divine providence was replaced by human vision. Hegel and his followers sweep the concept of process and progress into their philosophy of history and nature. No longer does there exist an external principle of justice in the universe, no longer a transcendent future. Both realities reside within the progressive unfolding of *Weltgeist—Weltgeschichte ist Weltgericht* for Hegel. There is no principle of judgment except the intrinsic process. Marx interprets this insight of intrinsic dialectic and process in economic and materialistic terms, completing the process of theomorphizing history and making a god of corporate humanity.

Proudhon, who also glories in the legacy of the French revolution, reads the chronicle of history as the human struggle against oppressive divine and ecclesiastical supremacy. Whereas Christianity has only replaced fate with the idea of providence, now our task is "defatalization"—a total rejection of any order that would define our future and delimit the affirmation of a free and open possibility.

Science and technology flourish against the backdrop of this mentality. All the great inventions of the eighteenth and nineteenth century are released in this consciousness. The years following Britain's "glorious revolution" and the decades prior to the French revolution witness a flurry of inventions, including the water flame, spinning jenny, power loom, and copying lathe. The steamboat, railroad, and internal combustion engine, as well as

the wide spectrum of working machines—all represent the irresistible human march forward. "Railroad iron is a magician's rod,"
wrote Ralph Waldo Emerson, "in its power to evoke the sleeping
energies of land and water . . . the development of our American
internal resources, the extension of the utmost of the commercial
systems, and the appearance of new moral causes which are to
modify the state, are giving an aspect of greatness to the future,
which the imagination fears to open." [74] In the late nineteenth and
early twentieth centuries, theology also becomes enamored with
the idea of inevitable human progress. Various utopian movements express the religious hope of realizing the kingdom of God
on earth. [75] The names of Schleiermacher, Ritschl, Harnack, and
Weiss are associated with this movement. "The idea of the Kingdom of God consists of those who believe in Christ, inasmuch as
they treat one another with love, without regard to differences of
sex, rank, or race, thereby bringing about a fellowship of moral
attitude and moral properties, extending through the whole range
of human life in every possible variation." [76]

The identification was too easy, however. Only the next decades
of cataclysmic world history could rescue biblical eschatology and
its necessary and salutary effect on human consciousness and conscience. Indeed, in the late nineteenth century, the apocalyptic
vision is retained by fierce and proud atheists like Proudhon,
Marx, and Nietzsche. "Schleiermacher's ethics," says Pannenberg,
"sees human reason perfectly capable of grasping the truth and
the good, so that his dominance over nature permits him to utilize
nature increasingly as a tool and as a symbol of his own destiny.
. . . The motif is humankind's acquisition of the world." What is
neglected in this mood of thought is the ambivalence of humanity's noblest objectives and design as the ultimate limitation of our
knowledge and skill. It remained for the terrible human and technological holocausts of the twentieth century to finally persuade
humanity that "within the reach of human action, there is no defi-
nite resolution of the human predicament." [77]

In 1919, amid terrifying historical crisis, Karl Barth wrote *Der
Romerbrief*, only slightly more than a decade after the appearance
of Albert Schweitzer's *The Mystery of the Kingdom of God*. In the

latter work, humankind is reminded of the fact that Jesus' teaching of the Kingdom is radically God-centered and God-directed. There is no delusion regarding humankind's capacity to fashion its own paradise. Schweitzer radically eschatologizes the New Testament message so that Jesus' teaching has only futuristic and personalistic meaning. Barth's work, in a similar vein, calls into question the whole development of natural theology and faith in human progress that characterizes nineteenth-century optimism. Christianity is eschatology, according to Barth: "If Christianity be not altogether restless eschatology, there remains in it no relationship whatever with Christ." [78] In Barth's relocation of eschatology at the heart of the Christian message, responsibility is emphasized. To wait for the kingdom of God and make ready for judgment is to take the kingdom of God with appropriate seriousness. This Kingdom, in terms of "end-history," is always near. It is always coming and is always present. It is qualitatively different from humankind's achievement, always remaining over against itself. "At the frontier of all time, before the overhanging wall of God, which signifies the abolition of all time and all content of time, stands the human of the 'last hour,' the human who awaits the Parousia of Christ." [79]

In Romans 8, humanity is saved by hope, not achievement. As humans wait for God and respond in hope to the future God brings, they are faithful. The genius of the human mind and manufacture is not inevitably its salvation. In the 1930s and 1940s, we learned this not only through rediscovering the New Testament, but also through the brutal lessons of the battlefield. Mustard gas, germ warfare, gun-laying mechanisms, and nuclear weaponry signal, if anything, the terrifying ambivalence of human progress. At the same time, the salutary features of the biomedical project were to unfold: antibiotics, immunizations, life-saving surgery, healings for the mind, and a commitment to social welfare.

Despite the resurgence of technological optimism in the post-war West, the critical ethical insight of the early decades of our century remains. Every proposal for some new Utopia is countered by a skeptical question. Youth culture today, in expressing antitechnocratic spirit, reflects this healthy wariness regarding human schemes and solutions. When Greenpeace ships thwart French nuclear testing, or when the Rand Corporation's computer design for a military *coup d'état* is disclosed, when pristine nature becomes Grenoble, Bhopal, or the Wales oil spill, our ethical consciousness shudders, despite the technological impressiveness. This is the awakened ethical spirit captured in the revival of biblical eschatology. Postmodernism and critical consciousness (e.g., conscientization, Paulo Freire) at best is rooted in the spirit of iconoclasm, prophecy, and proleptic hope in the biblical tradition.

The Second Assembly of the World Council of Churches, meeting in 1954 in my hometown, Evanston, Illinois, chartered this biblical vision of Christian hope amid the ambivalent aspirations of the new age. The commission to draft the main-theme document, "Christ: The Hope of the World," included Karl Barth, Emil Brunner, T. S. Eliot, Josef Hromadka, and Reinhold Niebuhr. A brief examination of the document is instructive regarding the early modern understanding of eschatology. The document stresses at the outset that human hope rests in God and comes from God: "What is spoken of here is something that we wait for expectantly and yet patiently, because we know that it can never disappoint us."[80]

Since our hope comes from the righteous God, it therefore is accompanied by judgment and repentance. "It is the crucified Lord who is the hope of the world."[81] Human hope is pursued under the sign of the cross. That is, "We are stripped naked of all our claims and pretensions and clothed afresh with His mercy."[82] In God, we who were dead are made alive again. God is our hope. We therefore do not face an aimless wandering in our future. "We face not a trackless waste of unfilled time with an end that none can dare to predict."[83] "He who has come and is coming . . . will reign for ever and ever."[84] Because he promises a new heaven and a new earth, "He promises seedtime and harvest as long as the earth remains, and gives men visions of a day when the disorders of life shall be done away, and righteousness, truth, and peace shall prevail."[85]

Although we have the Kingdom as its power is given in Christ, we know that humankind and nature are not yet what God would have them be. "Both are still enmeshed in the disorder of the unredeemed age and await their liberation."[86] Evil is "deeply ingrained and powerfully operative in all creation."[87] This, together with the perennial malice of humankind, expressed in "individual and corporate aggression, deceit and irresponsible self-seeking bedevils the whole course of earthly history."[88]

Our hope is not seen, or it would not be hope. It appears in the poetry of faith symbols. "Blind eyes will see, deaf ears will hear, the lame will leap for joy, the captive will be freed, we shall be changed, the dead will be raised incorruptible. The knowledge of God will cover the earth."[89] This world is captured within, yet not identifiable with God's coming Kingdom. "At the Cross, God condemned the world which turns from God and hates God. In the coming Day, a day of terrible finality, this condemnation will be at the same cross where God accepted the world and disclosed toward it unending and unqualified love. Confidence in this terrible and glorious consummation of all things in Christ means neither that the history of this world will be swept aside as irrelevant, nor that our efforts will be finally crowned with success. The long history of the world is not rendered meaningless by the coming of God's Kingdom. Nor is God's Kingdom simply the final outcome of this world's history."[90]

The Christian, therefore, cannot accept an understanding of history as a spiral of inevitable advance (democratic, scientific, Marxist, humanistic) or decline (modern despair). The Christian, rather, engages in earthly tasks "serving God and serving humankind."[91] Efforts for justice, freedom, and peace will be rewarded by God, whose will is redemption and release of humankind on the earth. We will not "confuse our programmes with God's Kingdom. We must still pray 'God be merciful to me a sinner.' "[92]

Although half a century later, the document bears too great a Niebuhrian influence, reflecting the pessimistic realism of Eliot's *Wasteland,* the essential ingredients of the Christian hope are articulated. The task for the church today is to forge those practical, technological tasks, promoted by hope and always bounded by the parameters of judgment and grace. The human project of securing well-being is framed by these boundaries.

We mentioned the modern revolutionary consciousness regarding the future. To this point we must return. The series of revolutions unleashed in the modern world, beginning with the French and American, continuing in the Russian and Chinese, and culminating in the recent liberation movements in Africa, Latin America, and Asia, signal an important development in the unfolding human consciousness. Revolutionary history can be interpreted in terms of the legacy of Christian history (Vander Leeuwen, Rosenstock-Huessy), or as an attempt to struggle with the contradiction within that history, as something discontinuous and new emerges. The notion that in this history, eschatology is secularized and human hope displaced from the transcendent kingdom of God into the temporal human possibility, is easily documented.

A critical estimate of this history is ventured by Michael Polanyi. Profoundly influenced by the inhuman, nihilistic spirit of modern life witnessed in the crush of Hungarian (1956) and Czech (1967) revolutions, he writes that we suffer today from an intensification of morality that is destroying the ethical foundations of our civilization. The whole history we have traced in this chapter is seen as a process of humans assuming a fiercer and more violent messianism as they assume control of their own destiny. The passions of the European revolutions did not indeed achieve the goals desired (Liberty, Equality, Fraternity); rather, they fashioned a messianic nationalism that could destroy a Semitic subculture or devastate a continent in the name of progress.[93]

In a similarly critical yet somewhat more romantic mood, Rosenstock-Huessy interprets the sequence of "revolutions of Christianity." In the Russian revolution, every proletarian is made a capitalist (within one economy held together by the Communist party). The French revolution makes every man of talent an aristocrat (within an invisible nation). The English revolt makes a king of every gentleman (within the United Kingdom). The German Reformation makes every man a priest (only in the universal religion). The revolutions at millennium's end exhilarate, while expropriating wealth and well-being from the poor. In other words, each revolution turns against itself, falls to conservatism, because it is fashioned by humans. "The majestic rhythm of the Great Revolutions of Christianity is characterized by its lack of arbitrary additions or omissions."[94]

The warnings of Polanyi and Rosenstock-Huessy again remind us of the necessity of acknowledging limitations to our titanism. Polanyi calls for humility based on sensible nationalism. Barth calls for a faith based on awe and devotion to the Lord of history. In each view, human energetic designs are tempered and sobered by an ethical sensitivity, making the human aware of what he can be and therefore should do.

The modern scientific and ethical consciousness emerges with this kind of moderation. In physics, Heisenberg's indeterminacy and Einstein's relativity theories have challenged humankind's notions of assured predictability and comprehensibility, from a spatial and temporal perspective. Subatomic physics and the new astronomy have opened vast vistas of unknown possibility that awe the human imagination. Weizsäcker goes so far as to argue for a new consideration of Spirit in relation to matter.[95] One consequence of the new consciousness is the high importance given to imagination and fantasy. Although technical reason is still linked with theoretical reason,[96] making ever-present the danger of direct connection between Oppenheimer's lab and the Enola Gay over Hiroshima, a new emphasis is placed on creative intuition and vision. In this sense, modern technical consciousness is imbued with a greater ethical sense than the early mind governed by Newtonian regularity, or the early modern mind fascinated with things (Fromm).

Youth today, the most sophisticated scientific generation ever to live, affirms what appears to be a new mysticism of nature. Fantasy and play are important in scientific theory, as in science-fiction imagination. They are also aspects of lifestyle. Youth, says Kenneth Keniston, seek "some consoling contact with objects and things, contact more immediate and embracing than afforded by daily experience. . . . They exhibit the unconscious desire to lose all selfhood in some undifferentiated state or another with nature."[97] If this mysticism is seen to be uncritical, it must be remembered that Einstein and Oppenheimer exhibited mystical tendencies late in life, Da Vinci's last drawings were of the deluge, and after 1692, Newton devoted the rest of his life to the study of prophecy.

The modern consciousness, both technical and ethical, has been formed by a long and varied history. The Christian view of future, of last judgment, of hope and promise, of the kingdom of God, has constituted an important pattern in this fabric. As we indicated at the outset, the important insight of Christianity is that the future is open, that possibility rather than fate controls the future, that God, a power of the future, guarantees its ethical quality and therefore demands human responsibility.

The contemporary insight proceeding from this tradition is that humankind's technical quest must be ethically expressed as creativity ever tempered by humility, as they stand before God's impending Kingdom. Polak is absolutely correct when he states that theology must accept the fact that "the future of the earth is still largely open and that the hour of collective, purposive, and scientifically recreative human power, free and volitional, to affect sociohistorical (and technical) events has at long last irrevocably struck." He is wrong to conclude that "the historical future of the earth from of old to the present day is not God's work but purely the work of humankind."[98] The history of the earth is humankind's history, as is its future, because it is God's history and future. Humans saw in their freedom, creativity, and hope the image of God. More important, humankind is not left to the limited discernments of its own wisdom, because the future bears the ethical power of the kingdom of God. Human ethical consciousness can respond to this reality and its technical vision and act accordingly.

The kingdom of God, the Hour of Christ, is an ever-temporal reality. It speaks to humankind in the depths of existential moment, in the trauma of historical events, and in the dynamic processes of nature.

When Baal was shown to be no power, Hebrew faith received the God of History, and nature was demythologized. When the Greek Pantheon collapsed, nature was again disenchanted. Now, in the coming of Christ, nature is given its rightful significance as the object of God's love and humankind's creativity. Nature is at once the object of humankind's *care*ful technical utilization and God's infinite purpose. All nature and history are captured in the eschatological power of God. Human knowledge, adoration, and responsibility are evoked by God, who wills that we know and work and cooperate in God's yet unfulfilled task of redemption.

We have surveyed the soil, or perhaps the landscape, from which technological consciousness emerges. An attempt has been made to show the way in which ethical consciousness, a perception of propriety and value, precedes and accompanies this consciousness. We have examined our cache of ideas, ideals, and beliefs that make us the people we are. To further our argument, we must now explicate the normative axioms and concrete values that can be derived from this composite worldview.

– CHAPTER THREE –

Derivative Ethical Axioms

Progress in Time and Measured Momentum

Primitive and premodern humanity waited for the future to come. Humankind was powerless to avert its threat or alter its possibility. Postmodern humanity, the full arbiter over truth and value, now creates the future. Hope and technology have joined in an accelerated human effort to fashion a new world in time and nature. Humans are not satisfied to leave it to chance; rather, we conceive of most reality, even life, health, and death, as being in the realm of our decisive control. We predict and plan births and deaths; well-being is shaped by cultural systems such as education, health care, and Social Security. We now measure the future, prognosticate our desires either by innovation or extrapolation, then program activities to realize our objectives. We live in the age of cyberspace. Virtual reality is our primary reality.

In this chapter, we will prepare a normative framework for evaluating technological efforts in the specific realm of life and health. Various goals of the project for well-being seek to direct the biological future of humanity. The unique element in today's programs is that they seek the tangible from the transcendent. They devolve back on our consciousness of time, history, and consummation, the values consciousness that were yielded to modern humanity by Judaism.

We have noted how Hebrew thought gives rise to the time consciousness that expresses itself in the modern ideas of progress. In the modern world, the idea of progress is injected with a certain sense of urgency. This time understanding is expressed in terms of guiding the future according to human intentions, rather than leaving it to nature and chance. Existent nature and fatality, especially in the realm of disease and death, is an evil not to be accepted, a condition to be changed. The ethical content in human consciousness that arises from Hebrew faith focuses on four areas: time (history), the natural world (including biological, sexual, procreative nature), humanity, and God. In each of these sectors of reality, an array of ethical principles and specific moral axioms can be derived from the Hebrew theological tradition. Let us explore, in turn, these four realms of ethical conviction and action.

Time

Time limits possibility because, due to the limitations of the frame in which human hope is projected into action, we are forced to accommodate our optimal desires into practical possibilities. As in the words of Bruce Springsteen's moving ballad at the end of the film *Dead Man Walking:* "Between our dreams and actions is the world." The limitations of time force our eschatological visions into realizable wishes. The desire to accomplish urgent change is both the glory and the tragedy of humanity. Polanyi argues that the outbreak of "moral fervor" unleashed in the modern world has not only "achieved numberless humanitarian reforms, but has in our own lifetime, outreached itself by its inordinate aspirations and thus heaped on humankind the disasters that have befallen us." [1]

The terrifying ambivalence of history should be enough to remind us of the danger inherent in our technological action. We continue, however, to assert our mastery over time and drive more and more recklessly toward our destruction. The modern idea of progress, though rooted in Jewish and Christian consciousness, also bears aspects of a pagan denial of God that drives humans in accelerated madness toward a goalless oblivion. Weizsäcker, with his Hellenic penchant, goes so far as to suggest that scientific humanity has made a god of time:

> The pathos of endless progress which drives on modern physics and
> technology transfers a predicate of God (Time) to the world and
> turns toward time as no pagan has ever done, but as the Christian
> turns to that eternity which has appeared in the midst of history.[2]

Whereas the fully secularized idea of progress, with its correlate of time acceleration, allows no parameters of meaning and
purpose, the Jewish and Christian understanding of time bears
principles of purpose which signal ethical axioms. It is the purpose
of this chapter to locate those axioms and show that the roots of
modern time consciousness rest in a theological tradition which
also conveys normative insight. If our present and future technical
assessment and planning insist on the modern negation of these
roots, the consequences will be grave.

Theologically considered, the future has moral quality which
bears to us the insight as to what it should become. To use
Kierkegaard's image, we can row backward into an unknown
future, anticipating it to be sheer novelty and capriciousness.
Although the Christian hope for the future is based on novelty,
this consciousness now prompts us to row forward into history, in
a sense confident of its direction and purpose because it is
enfolded in the providence of God. The substantive hope of the
community of Hebrews in world history is for protection of life
and health, and diminution of the forces that disease, injure, and
kill human beings. The tradition affirms longevity, procreativity,
physical and mental well-being, and the fuller expression of
human potential.

Psychically, humans are forward-leaning creatures. We are the
"hopers."[3] Our "leaning into the future" is heightened through
our evolutionary advance and the development of our central nervous system. "The more human we are," writes René Dubos, "the
more intensely do our anticipations of the future affect the character of our responses to the forces of the present."[4] The high
incidence of anxiety and neurosis in the modern world can be
accounted for also on this basis. Human hopes both lengthen in
the time horizon and intensify in the time frame. Human expectations take on an urgency that releases both high creative and
destructive energy.

Expectation, intention, anticipation, premonition, and presentiment—all these have a forward reference in time. Our entire psychic life is permeated with the hope of things to come, which is the counterpart of nostalgia for the past. Implicit in all our actions are plans, however vague and inarticulate, for the future, and sometimes, as in saving our investment, this planning is deliberate. As we ascend the evolutionary scale, the temporal horizon becomes more and more extended. This may be illustrated by the fact that delay may be increased at higher phylogenetic levels; the rat can sustain a delay of some 4 minutes, the cat 7 hours, and the chimpanzee 48 hours. In us the horizon may reach beyond our own brief existence; from infancy onward there is a growing capacity to relate what is happening at the moment to events foreshadowed in the more distant future.[5]

Three ethical axioms can be derived from Hebrew time consciousness in its emphasis on nature as history and on humans as responsible creatures of destiny. The first principle concerns the historicity of nature; the second, the viability of reason; the third, the vitality of hope. If humanity and nature are caught up in God's time process, (a) humans are therefore responsible to direct natural evolution according to God's righteousness. Second, (b) the acceleration of technology must be measured and limited by the controlling parameter of knowledge and wisdom. Finally, (c) humans are responsible for affirming an endless time horizon. We *ought* to affirm and work on that which we believe redeems and is reasonable and endures.

(a) We have emphasized the revolutionary element in Hebrew consciousness, not yet fully realized, that nature is not an eternal cyclic entity, but a historic process. All nature, including human nature, is caught up in the historical process. This means that nature has a developmental quality. It is becoming something; and humans must choose to inform and direct that process or, negatively, decide to "let nature run its course." Humanity, possessed with Hebrew consciousness, knows nature to be part of the redemptive time process of the Creator. Humans now know that nature drives toward its destiny not only with Darwinistic evolutionary struggle, but with the purposive energy stimulated by its Creator. The earth moves toward that glorious salvation of the world as depicted in the Apollinaris mosaic in Ravenna, the *Consummatio Mundi.*

In this view, humans are prompted to direct the evolution of nature, as far as our capacities allow, in a moral direction. The woods and forests of the highly developed nations, for example, have developed completely under human guidance. Though wilderness and prairie, rainforest and *terra nullus*, have their inherent beauty and value, were humans to withdraw their tending care, the forests would grow into untamed chaos, useless for any purpose. The great evil of our time, of course, is the misuse of this taming capacity and responsibility. In the microbiological sphere, the world of germs and fungi has to be checked in vaccination and antibiotic therapy, all the while respecting the autonomy and natural value of this universe of life. To rightly direct the evolutionary development of microbe and plant, fossil fuel, and mineral and water development will require highly disciplined care in the near future, lest nature collapse into chaos.

Humans also have the responsibility to control their own evolution. Here we must see that our future does not overwhelm us. We must energetically develop the biological adaptations, even the genotypic and phenotypic alterations required to cope in the future we are creating. As Wolf Dieter Marsch has remarked, "the evolution of homo sapiens must be regarded as a function of his technology."[6] This does not mean resignation to the necessity of an increasingly toxic environment, prompting us to build people with biological built-in gas-mask prostheses. Rather, it means a delicate attention to the future of both nature and the needs of the human species, working those subtle transformations of each that will guide the future with justice and righteousness. Those agricultural transformations (the green revolution) that enable the starving to eat, to mature and develop, to find creative energy for life's tasks, are one example of this. Pesticides and genetically engineered crops have their downside, but their salutary benefit has been overwhelming. Similarly, the biological transformations (e.g., insulin management of diabetes), though not without significant feedback consequences, increase the facility of the human family to survive and cope.

The normative guidelines of justice and righteousness are those discernments within which we know what humanity and nature should become. The perceptions disclose what now is wrong (e.g., infant mortality from malnutrition, the obliteration of CO_2 photosynthesizing plants) and engender anger in the knowledge of what should and could be. Justice in Hebrew faith is not retaliation or "getting what one deserves," certainly not "survival of the fittest," but rather a positive quality of life, where fulfillment and peace reign because humans, in blessed reciprocity with the entire natural world, serve the divine glory.

The surest practical guideline of this ethical principle is that technology most surely pursues its moral possibility as it serves the needs of the poor and the weak. When it heals the sick, feeds the hungry, shelters the exposed, binds together those separated, it anticipates the kingdom of God. Teilhard was fond of speaking of nature as a process of eschatological becoming, within which humankind cooperates, straining with God toward the fulfillment of nature. Humans have the time responsibility of hastening and instrumentally facilitating, not stalling this righteous process.

(b) Silence and waiting are the complementary grace of urgent action. When the mechanical clock was invented in the West, it was put inside the churches and church towers to remind the people of the regularity of God's ways. It was a sermon commending people to carefully measure time as the Creator purportedly does. In the East, before the Marxist state, one never saw a clock in the church. When in the seventeenth century, an Englishman on the Czar's order built a clock over Savior's Gate at the Kremlin, the faithful Russian peasant reacted violently. The eternal Jerusalem had been contaminated by time (*chronos*). In the West, however, time soon became the measure of eternity and the master of humanity.[7]

The furious acceleration that begins with the enlightenment idea of progress and rushes into our own technological age must be tempered by wisdom. At the outset of his book *Designing the Future,* Robert Prehoda paints a panorama of breathtaking innovations that may come in the next few decades, if we act fast enough. Direct 3-D color television-telephones, human cloning, human-computer symbioses to relieve tired brains, and a vast array of technological wonders are within human grasp. "All of the advances . . . are likely to be achieved by humankind. The question is, when can we accelerate the process that will permit their early realization?"[8] For Prehoda, as for many other technology enthusiasts, the future has an uncertainty and unpredictability about it. This gives rise to premonitions of danger, which in turn increase the desire for immediate action. The time urgency is based on a view that "if we do not do something quick, it will be too late."

In Hebrew consciousness we are aware of the limits that wisdom places on sheer acceleration for acceleration's sake. The Lord speaks to Job:

> "Where were you when I laid the foundations of the earth . . . or who shut up the sea with doors . . . who causes it to rain upon the earth . . . who provides the raven its food. . . . Shall he that argues with the Almighty instruct him?" (Job 38–40 RSV)

In wisdom, God has fashioned the earth, set its boundaries, founded its processes and energies. In a silent faithlike quality, humans perceive the wisdom behind and within nature as the wise purpose of God. Time will not run out of control, nor will nature rush ahead unconstrained, because time and nature are governed by divine wisdom. In the great recension that climaxes the Noahic deluge, humanity is promised that times and seasons will remain while earth endures (Genesis 8:22).

God's eternity invests time with meaning. The process of change into future is not random and pointless, but invested with undergirding purpose. Toffler has shown how sheer momentum creates only *Future Shock.* Momentum with meaning is a progress that is founded on wisdom. "A future without eternity amounts to meaningless change," writes Pannenberg. "If people are exposed to an essentially empty future, future shock results, because meaningless change endangers our personal identity."[9]

Scientific investigations and inventions reveal a wondrous momentum in time. Consider the development of Beta and Calcium channel blockers in the care of those with heart disease. So much foundational knowledge, both physiological and pharmacological, had to accrue before "the time was ripe." Then when "the time was fully come," the breakthrough came with an urgency and inevitability. The value of waiting and working has transmuted into blessing in life. My own father is among a considerable community of persons who have gained significant years of good life.

(c) The final derivative axiom that we would locate in Hebrew time consciousness concerns the length of the human time horizon. The Hebrew poets and prophets knew God as the creator of unlimited time. When we sing the Gloria in the liturgy, the Anglican form "for evermore," "for ever and ever" more correctly connotes the Hebrew than the German intention. The meaning is temporal, not metaphysical. God has founded the earth from unlimited past and wills to carry it into the unlimited future.

Although by nature humans have a limited time horizon, in hope and faith we know of the enduring future of the earth and of our responsibility to ensure that lasting time. Physiologically and psychically, we may be impatient; socially, we may selfishly strive only to secure our own well-being. In response, we realize that we are created to work in the present as if the world should go on forever. While a scorching sun may bake the earth to death in two billion years, or while human heat released into the atmosphere may someday disturb the delicate balance of warmth and coolness, a purposive span of benevolent "for the time being" characterizes the history of the earth.

 A commitment to the future generations is problematic in traditional law because rights are based on the claims one party makes on another. Unborn generations, of course, can make no such claim. As in abortion policy, advocacy for the yet unborn can come only from sheer good will or grace-bestowed love. There is little chance that the virtue will be affirmed in self-interest. In a penetrating essay, Martin Golding, of the John Jay College of Criminal Justice in New York, locates this source: "We are all familiar with the kind of 'taking an interest in the welfare of another' that is gracious and gift-like, a matter of *noblesse oblige*."[10] Although still requiring grace, we can love those who reciprocally share our life, because we see them. The world of the future requires that mystic insight which without seeing, yet believes (John 20:29).

Jørgen Randers, of the M.I.T. systems analysis team, has called on the faith communities to invest our culture with the long time horizon.[11] In his argument, they alone have the resources to sustain a future vision beyond the immediate future. Our present mania for rapid economic growth and expansion is posited on a very short time scale (e.g., 50 years). We live out an ideology of planned obsolescence. The industrial planners have either a bland optimism toward the future (finding substitutes for fossil fuels, metals, oxygen, etc.) or a blatant disregard ("What did the future ever do for me?").

The Hebrew time view, which resides at the heart of Christian eschatology, and the mentality that gives birth to science and technology in the West, guards at once against fatalism and nihilism. Time does not grind incessantly toward destructive purpose, nor is it devoid of meaning. It is *Chronos*, in that it is constituted by spaces that are to be filled by human activities. It is *Kairos*, in that it has the capacity to bear the Word and Wisdom of the Creator who makes it. Humanity's task is to perceive the normative significance of time and bear out responsibly its brief allotment of life, as if it infinitely mattered.

Because of time, humans suffer and die. Because of history, the tragic is real. Yet time also makes hope and possibility, and therefore responsibility, real. Suffering indeed informs human hope and technological planning: "It is the suffering from the earthly anguish and unfree human conditions which this love recognizes," says Moltmann, "that wishes happiness for the poor and freedom for the humiliated and is, therefore, ready to make investments."[12] Chastened suffering, which is the meaning of the cross and the history of Jews, discloses not an omnipotent God who eternally surveys the temporal agony of humankind, but rather the God of love who joins Godself to human life in compassion (co-suffering) in time to fashion a new humanity, a new earth, a new creation.

Nature

The second ethical principle found in Hebraism is that Nature is the vehicle of divine purpose. In the exile prophet Isaiah, we find the whole Hebraic tradition focused on the issues of birth and death, health and life, aging and childhood:

> "For behold, I create new heavens and a new earth;
> and the former things shall not be remembered
>   or come into mind.
> But be glad and rejoice for ever
>   in that which I create;
> for behold, I create Jerusalem a rejoicing,
>   and her people a joy.
> I will rejoice in Jerusalem,
>   and be glad in my people;
> no more shall be heard in it the sound of weeping
>   and the cry of distress.
> No more shall there be in it
>   an infant that lives but a few days,
>   or an old man who does not fill out his days,
> for the child shall die a hundred years old,
>   and the sinner a hundred years old shall be accursed.
> They shall build houses and inhabit them;
>   they shall plant vineyards and eat their fruit.
> They shall not build and another inhabit;
>   they shall not plant and another eat;
> for like the days of a tree shall the days of my people be,
>   and my chosen shall long enjoy the work of their hands.
> They shall not labor in vain,
>   or bear children for calamity;
> for they shall be the offspring of the blessed of the LORD,
>   and their children with them.
> Before they call I will answer,
>   while they are yet speaking I will hear.
> The wolf and the lamb shall feed together,
>   the lion shall eat straw like the ox;

and dust shall be the serpent's food.
They shall not hurt or destroy
in all my holy mountain,
    says the LORD."
                (Isaiah 65:17-25 RSV)

What is the character and import of this ethical principle? God has created human beings designed for health and life, generativity and longevity. This blessed shalom has been distorted by a rebellion in the creation that is composed of human irresponsibility, by the inevitable deleterious consequences of freedom, and by inherent contradictions built into nature itself. People kill themselves and others by willful neglect and violence. For example, mothers consume drugs during pregnancy, injuring themselves and the children they carry. Societies fail to provide food, housing, and health care to poor pregnant mothers, and infant mortality increases. Second, in terms of freedom, accidents occur—children drink the kitchen lye, the child on the bicycle is struck by the bus—persons do not live out their lives. Finally, there is an irascible imperfection in the human organism that reflects the fracture in God's good world itself: There are genetic flaws—Down syndrome, cystic fibrosis, Tay-Sachs disease. There may even be some gene complex that determines aging and limits the life span. Is this a problem to be diagnosed and fixed? Is it a condition that is part of the excellence of the creation?

The ethical principle obliges us to accept the givens of nature while straining toward the eschatological perfections. We are commissioned to work for a world where children will not die prematurely, where sterility will not haunt the human family, where persons will not fail to live out their full life spans.

Humanity

Another central ethical principle of Hebrew faith is commitment to justice among the human family. Torah and the broader tanakh (*Torah, Navi'im, Kethuvim*)—indeed, the entire instructional and inspirational literature of Israel, calls humanity to human care, concern for the weak and oppressed, equality for all persons, respect for women, children, the aged, the stranger and despised one. The human tendency to cruelly crush the weak, to exploit the vulnerable or, more pervasively, to simply ignore those for whom life is filled with hurt, suffering, and frustration, is diametrically challenged by the biblical tradition. Secular stipulates of justice—equality, compensation, and the like—are enriched by the stipulates of mercy—outgoing positive love and concern for those in need. A range of practical axioms about life and health proceed from this ethical principle.

God

The revelation of God to Israel, and the derivative transformation of human ethical consciousness, ultimately sets a higher order of value and good over against human affirmations. Survival is a prime human value biologically and, according to Maslow's hierarchy of human desires, preeminent in the scale of value. Survival may not be God's will in particular circumstances. Even the finest theological values, not killing or stealing, may be suspended in the face of larger divine imperatives. Humans are always reminded

> For my thoughts are not your thoughts,
> neither are your ways my ways, says the LORD.
> (Isaiah 55:8 RSV)

The Parameters of Nature

The Greeks had a theatrical device by which a god, carried by some machine, would intervene in the drama to bring judgment or avert some calamity. Today we also trust in *deus ex machina*. On the one hand, some say that we should not contort and twist nature beyond its limits. In anthropomorphic terms, it is argued that nature will recoil in objection to our intrusion and set its own natural sanctions and limitations. To return to Hebrew morality—especially the natural law holiness tradition of Israel—it is argued that lack of hygienic vigilance will bring about infections, perhaps sexually transmitted diseases. Another example: a fruit fly population will multiply to a density at which it tests the carrying capacity of some bell-jar environment. Infertility and violence then occur to curb further population growth. The same will happen in human communities, it is claimed. Nature, which we have poisoned, will turn around and poison us. We will learn how far we can go. The *deus ex machina* here is not a savior but rather a boundary of nature—a border that continually reminds us of the limitations of our manipulative freedom.

With a similar fatalism, many contemporaries claim from a religious perspective that God will rescue humanity if we go too far. Either God will end the human story when we have hanged ourselves on the rope of self-destruction, or will use some great Noahic calamity to recall us to faithfulness.

Both these views express a confidence that there are natural or supernatural conditions that will rescue humans from the ultimate abuse of our freedom. Both opinions raise the question of whether there is some necessary or determined force at work that sets limits in nature, and in what respect this force lessens or deepens the demands of humankind's responsibility. As the Broadway show song goes, "plant a radish—get a radish" (from *Fantastiks*), or in biblical language, those who "sow to the flesh will from the flesh reap corruption" (Galatians 6:8).

In this section we will survey the evidence for the natural and supernatural parameters that exhibit the limits of human possibilities regarding our utilization of nature. Our purpose is to articulate ethical principles, which can then be applied through axioms to specific technological proposals. These proposals for future technological development contend that cautious fears of limitations are impediments to the great possibilities of humankind. Nature, it is argued, bears only the law of encouragement to the human quest. Nature, it is held, willingly discloses its secrets to our inquisitive intellect and bends to our manipulative designs. Nature responds rationally to our intellect and plastically to our technology. Nature will work against humanity only if we fail to dream and act imaginatively. We first will discuss the parameters of technological possibility inherent in nature. Then we will reevaluate what theology has traditionally called the "orders" of creation. Finally, we will derive two ethical principles concerning our utilization of nature in the light of human ecology within the divine economy.

In the widely discussed study *The Limits to Growth*, the authors examine numerous critical parameters, which when extrapolated into the future, begin to show the limits of nature's capacity to bear or absorb the results of human activity.[13] It is interesting to note that the parameters of limitation come not from the intrinsic principles of an eternal universe, but in the hard fact that we live in a finite cause-effect world. In the Club of Rome study, five major trends were observed: accelerating industrialization, rapid population growth, widespread malnutrition, depletion of nonrenewable resources, and a deteriorating environment. Each factor analyzed can be graphed in an exponential curve that rapidly ascends to a ceiling limitation. The use of arable land, for example, has increased so rapidly in the last decades that a major catastrophe can be expected in the next century, given a continued rate of utilization, regardless of new efficiencies.

Nature's limits, according to this approach, will confront humanity in terms of falling off curves when earth reaches her carrying capacity. As industrial growth accelerates, for example, environmental pollution absorption mechanisms become saturated. Pollution rises rapidly, precipitating an increasing death rate and decline in food production. Through the interaction of many variables, an inevitable process of correction sets in, so that nature's limits, having been ruptured, are restored to some equilibrium.[14]

Because of our dullness of mind and slowness to respond, nature sometimes discloses its wisdom in vivid cataclysm which it cannot avoid. The great death in London during the 1960s showed dramatically the insidious effects of air pollution that had been slowly building up in the environment. Unfortunately, it appears that we humans need such periodic catastrophes to bring us to our senses.

To distinguish the natural from the unnatural is most difficult. This dilemma is the crux of the controversy on birth control measures. Is the pill in its varied forms a device in harmony with nature's patterns or does it intrude another pattern that sooner or later will result in negative feedback? What of RU 486? Does it mimic nature's own *abortifacience*? Does the combination of methotrexate and misoprostol violate fundamental natural processes? Does it injure the organism for further conception? Is it natural or unnatural, good or evil?

It is important at this point to ask the question—what is natural? Scientists such as geneticist Dobzhansky have pointed out that human creativity is part of what we call nature. "One stands in bewilderment before a mentality that claims to know exactly what is natural and what is unnatural. Humankind has changed nature in innumerable ways and will doubtless continue doing so. It is, indeed, 'natural' for humankind to recast nature." [15]

The satisfactory resolution of this question will affirm that human attitudes and decisions become a part of natural process. Although, as Bertrand Russell has suggested, nature may grind relentlessly against any human purpose and value, humans somehow remain irresistibly stimulated by the dual imperative to change and control nature, and do it purposefully. The point at which we impose form, structures, and momentum inimical to nature's own qualities, is where our wisdom needs to be sharpened by an awareness of nature's wisdom.

Raising the question of human wisdom prompts us to look carefully at the human mania for growth. If any attitude on humanity's part lies at the essence of its misapplied technology, it is this. The economists, with few exceptions, have contended that human wants are insatiable, that it is human nature to crave more and better. Although Robert Theobald and others have questioned this assumption, it still underlies the economic policies of the nations of the world. [16] This mentality, rooted in the Protestant ethic where capitalism is joined to Puritanism, contends that limits are to be overcome, and progress is to spiral forward unendingly. During two expanding centuries, writes Geoffrey Vickers,

[we have] developed an implicit belief that the progress is an expanding one which will always call for and always evoke a further exercise of human domination over the environment and, with this metaphysical belief in the way things work, [we] have developed

the corresponding ethic, that dominance over nature is the distin-
guishing mark of humankind, that to transcend a limitation is
courageous and noble, to accept it is cowardly and base.[17]

It is as if the human quest is identical with greater and greater
accomplishment in a purely quantitative sense. Life gains its
meaning in overcoming limitations. One cannot think of a value
more basic to Western culture.

In our world of technological innovation, the analogy of nature's
wisdom may be just what we need. When we can conceive of
nature as an organism, with the intrinsic imperatives of harmony,
interdependence, and mutuality, we come very close to the Greek
natural wisdom which Paul the Apostle affirmed in his understanding of the body. Healthy growth in this normative insight is not
linear, certainly not exponential, but rather organismic, in the
sense that it proceeds within the given structural and temporal
forms. It takes each possibility, each creative potential to its fullest
expression. Let me give two good examples of this responsible
technical action. One would be the geodesic dome, utilizing what
Buckminster Fuller calls "anticipatory design," which sensitively
responds to the majestic harmonies of nature. Another might be
the Taconic State Parkway in lower New York state, which evoked
René Dubos' appreciation for the way it weaves gently along the
natural contours of that graceful landscape.

We are driven to the point of humankind's perception of
nature's good wisdom and its response to it in technical act. West-
erners have often wrested from resistant nature its purposes. Lynn
White, in his masterful studies of medieval technology, has drawn
an important contrast by use of the Western and Eastern icons. In
an interview at the World Council of Churches headquarters in
Geneva, he informally commented on the difference:

> In the Greek manuscripts pertaining to Humankind's Dominion,
> the pictures show Adam sitting in the Garden of Eden, quite
> possibly with the animals scattered around him. Sometimes in
> these Greek paintings, the hand of God appears from a cloud to
> bless the whole situation. The western pictures are very different in
> mood. God is standing with Adam and has seized Adam's arm in

God's left hand. With a very hortatory gesture, God is telling Adam exactly what should be done, now. There's an urgency about this which is totally lacking in the Greek pictures, and the poor animals are far from being relaxed. They are all huddled off in a corner looking scared—and in view of the long-term impact of the attitude reflected in these pictures, I think they have a right to look scared.[18]

Again my mind recalls the great Ravenna mosaic at St. Apollinaris on the salvation of the world. Here, to my recollection, the insights of East and West are blended in a great expression of Western-Byzantine faith. The Lord of creation is Jesus the Savior, depicted as a shepherd. The brilliant green landscape is the garden for the sheep and other beasts. The scene blends an eschatological pastoral with an earthly humanistic hymn of praise. Here humans are the tenants of the Creator's garden, responsible to adore and praise as they tend and create. The great dome, now called in Italian *"Transfigurazione,"* suggests that nature's deepest destiny is its transformation and beatification in the will of God through human instrumentality.

Responsible human creativity with nature, Carl Friedrich von Weizsäcker related in an interview, is the gentle blending of maintaining and transforming values. The Greeks achieved maintenance wisdom. It is at the heart of the Christian cosmology and anthropology. A new spirit of transformation is let loose as that Greco-Christian faith gives birth to modern science and technology. In the East today, the values of maintenance, of silence, listening, resignation to fate, are retained. Our prophetic youth sense the loss of this element in the West and hearken to Eastern religions. In the West, particularly in America, the value of transformation is stressed. Too frequently, it is change for the sake of power and profit, rather than transformation in an ethical sense. Both elements in our consciousness need to be recovered. If human life is to survive with meaning, it is necessary to delicately balance these imperatives.

Human dominion must always beware of the temptation toward domination and autonomy. Proper domination within nature is a responsible humility before God and a responsive relatedness to the earth, our fellow creature. Charles West has said: "We are empowered by God to have dominion over other forms of life and our environment, but the built-in limit of this power is from the beginning the calling to bring forth the fruits of the earth and to respond to the call of God to fulfill God's promise in relation with us." [19]

We have discussed the limits of nature and the moral contours of nature as offering normative value. The study of such limits and norms has generally been gathered under the theme of natural law or orders of creation. These norms have traditionally pertained to natural, political, and familial goods. In natural-law ethics, we address matters such as environment, the state, war and peace, family, sexuality, procreation, and dying. Let us now turn to the traditional theological understanding of these themes.

Although the Greek influence on Christian theology has come under much needed criticism,[20] the Greek wisdom expressed in the Christian doctrine of orders is worthy of reconsideration. Thomas Aquinas appropriated Greek insight through Aristotle into his theology. The thought of Luther and Calvin does not fundamentally alter this classic system regarding the orders of creation and of human life. The Lutheran tradition amplifies the thought of emergency orders as being part of creation orders, leading to some later distortions of the importance of the secular. God, it is contended, has established the rules for life. These rules have been violated. Now, after the Fall, a more rigorous dispensation of judgment and grace has been set in place. The rigor almost brings a discontinuity into the moral life. Calvin stresses the transparency of nature, through which God reveals God's glory and renders humans responsible. There is still natural goodness in the nation, family, love and parenting, health, living and dying. This composite tradition retains the Greek structure of thought with its positive element of wisdom, as well as its negative element—a deprecation of history. Ultimately, life in the body passes away. Only eternity endures.

The concept of orders based on the Greek metaphysic affirmed the structures of human nature to have a permanence and normative inviolability. Marriage, family, community, church, vocation, and culture were examples of orders. There were also special orders related to extraordinary features of the divine economy and emergency orders (Noahic covenant), designed to restrain sin and organize life in the interim between Fall and eschaton. In the same way the wisdom of nature is reflected in her limits, the wisdom of God for human life is expressed in God's ordinances. The essence of the insight is that God has informed human life with certain capacities, certain possibilities, and certain responsibilities. The image of God taking human expression in the person of Jesus as Christ expresses the contours of human being, the boundaries within which our possibility and responsibility must take place. The great questions of transforming human nature—the human-machine chimera, brain modification, rebuilding humans, genetic engineering—all can be viewed in this normative context.

In Aquinas, the orders are rooted in pure natural law. In the modern Catholic tradition, the meaning is retained, although theologians speak more of intrinsic meanings and purposes. In contemporary Protestant thought, we speak of the "island of natural law in the ebb and flow of positive law" (Ellul), or of "unchangeable basic structures" (Brunner), or the "conditions of humankind's historical life" (Althaus), or the "limits of humanity" (Thielicke). Each of these approaches attempts to establish that which is inviolable and fundamental to humans qua humans. As created beings, we are subject to the fates of finitude and the force of destiny. In Sartre's phrase, we are condemned to freedom. As creatures made in God's image, we share the divine capacities of knowledge, moral awareness, memory, and hope in the moral sense. As the redeemed humanity in Jesus Christ, we have become the friend of God—cooperators in ongoing creation and victors over the destructive forces of sin and death. We are released to the capacities of care and friendship, and the range of graces called Gifts of the Spirit.

In Protestant thought, the orders have come to be interpreted in a moral rather than a naturalistic sense. Brunner saw the ordinances as a "sphere of life . . . within which God's will meets us." Bonhoeffer refers to the principles of meaning that inform the human reality as "mandates." Mandates, says Moltmann, "are not eternal structures of human existence but rather historical functions of God's active lordship." [21] They are not unreal and transitory but eschatological, in the sense that they convey a purpose far greater than the immediate reality. As Bonhoeffer said, "they extend to the borders of time."

The orders generally refer to the social and cultural expressions of human life. Important for us is the meaning they bear for the limits of personal being and existence. Do humans violate their humanity when linked to a computer? When our behavior is chemically modified? When we are linked to a machine for space work? When we are tied cybernetically to life-support systems? The contemporary relevance of the theological insight into orders is simply that nature and human nature have limits, contours which establish the shape and development of their possibility; moral determinants that indicate what each should become and therefore what distortion should not be tolerated. Strangely enough, this classic insight is collaborated in the empirical evidence of what is now happening to nature and to human nature. The blue ocean growing gray and the terror of mental illness may be signals that we have gone too far, or perhaps that we have not come far enough. The fact that the two dominant diseases afflicting humankind early in the twenty-first century will be AIDS and Alzheimer's causes us to morally pause and reflect on our rupture of nature. A modern anthropology of orders would contend that all alterations bear the option of enhancing humanity's intrinsic possibility or reducing it to subhumanity. The criterion of discernment rests with the answer to the question, what does it (technicalization) do for "keeping human life human" (Lehmann) in liberating all our capacities, and how does it sharpen in our consciousness the perception of and free choice of the divine mandate? How does this or that alteration enhance our human facility to adore our Maker and serve our fellow human beings?

We can now assert two ethical principles from the foregoing analysis. One concerns the wisdom of nature reflected in what we might call parameters of technological possibility. The other concerns the boundaries of human being. Both insights are derivative from the Greek consciousness. They convey values for two representative schemes of proposed technological development which we shall alter analysis. First we affirm that: (a) Nature's wisdom should be accepted in human utilization of its resources and energies, so that our definitions of the good life for global humanity are tempered by the value of eco-harmony; (b) Humans should strive to perfect their nature, removing the impediments to wholeness and fulfillment, and exploring all the possibilities that express our best. But we always should remain cognizant of the fact that we are unique children of a God who entertains our cooperation in a cosmic drama of transfiguration, a God who gives us to be the brothers and sisters of all earth's people, now and into the future.

(a) Humans should listen sensitively to the natural rhythms of nature and see our function of stewardship as promoting the evolutionary wisdom of nature's development. Yet nature's innermost purpose is to fulfill the designs of God, whose will is the healing reconciliation and abundant life for that global human family that God has fashioned in God's image. Humanity should not retreat, therefore, to some romantic wilderness existence, or be satisfied with some static state where growth and development grind to a halt, and the imperatives of release of the full potential of global humanity and equitable distribution of the good earth's resources remain unaccomplished. We are given to the world to build the earth toward its inherent intention (Teilhard de Chardin). Human creativity, responsibility offered, is natural and good. Indeed, humans are necessary for the world's wholesome propensities to be realized.

(b) Regarding the transformation of our own being, we should acknowledge the scientific and theological wisdom that we have not yet become what we shall be. The evolutionary history of the human species is extremely short. The rational and ethical possibilities inherent in our nature are poignantly expressed in the tragic history that discloses our immature and penultimate state. The clear meaning of the great crisis that characterizes modern life is that humanity and the enfolding cosmos groans and travails toward some new possibility. Human ingenuity should gently, respectfully, and reverently move toward these potentials.

The moral genius of the natural-law tradition is obvious. It seeks to conform and coincide human creativity and activity to the given patterns, rhythms, and causalities by which nature operates. The weaknesses of the orientation are also evident. It leads toward quiescence and conservation. Both human creativity and a true reading of the physical world and its processes show that natural law, especially when applied to human and social affairs, is as much an arbitrary and imposed structure of the human mind on reality as it is an immovable law. Feudal social structure can become a divine and natural truth. Postmodern criticism helpfully shows the relativity of such conceptions.

Yet we finally must be aware that we can destroy ourselves by abrupt and radical alteration of nature; we must avoid the danger, on the one hand, of considering our present state as the final perfection. The great eugenic proposals (sperm banks, for example) argue as fundamental value that we should ensure that people to come after us ought to be like we are. This is arrogant presumption. On the other hand, we should not be so dissatisfied with our present state of development that we see any and all change as desirable. The biological proposals we shall next review—the human genome project, for example—disparage humanity in our present limitation and seek to rush us prematurely into some supposedly superior state. It is a natural and spiritual grace to simultaneously accept what one presently is as good, and yet strain to that new possibility carried in the wisdom of one's technical and ethical consciousness. The human quest should be marked by grateful, glad contentment with what is—along with a vibrant hope for what could be.

The Impulses of Creativity and Discontent

The ethical fervor characteristic of apocalyptic consciousness is alive again today. As Elaine Pagels has shown, the symbolic matrix of good/evil is a projection of the human psyche *against* powers of evil and any affirmation of salutary projects in order to ameliorate human pain and enhance health. Objective powers also imprint that same dialectic on human consciousness. Dynamics of good and evil are vivid and intense as the human race moves toward the end of the second millennium of the Christian (common) era. The times seem to quake with both despair and expectation. The vibrancy of the human project is great—accelerating with restless momentum. It is quite evident that we are entering an age where old patterns will yield to the new and unexpected. We tremble and yet anticipate the prospects. Strangely enough, however, the ethical zeal inciting action, always present in apocalyptic awareness, is accompanied today by a passivity and pessimism, perhaps shaped by affluent hedonism and cyberspace. The twofold attitudinal consciousness of expectant waiting and energetic predictive activity are present dramatically in historical "times of troubles." It may be that our age is preapocalyptic. If so, we need to weigh the ethical imperatives implicit in such consciousness to see how they relate to our contemporary problems.

The apocalyptic literature is at once a literature of despair and hope. Resting as it does on the yet to be fulfilled promises of God and the terror of the present tribulation, it provokes an ethic that blends the seemingly paradoxical elements of creativity and discontent. Although it is true that apocalyptic movements stand at the edge of what might be called the "normative center" of Jewish-Christian tradition, the combination of intensified prophetic and predictive insight in this consciousness is most critical to our thesis. In planning and assessing our technology, we are concerned not only with descriptive tasks, but with the search for insights into what is wrong with the present, where the future holds threat and promise, and how we should appropriate the good possibility and achieve that desirable future.

Consider the current concern with environmental deterioration, for example. The mood today is certainly apocalyptic. One hears repeated warnings that we soon shall witness the cataclysmic obliteration of one age and the abrupt initiation of another, if there is anything left. In these concerns, one hears the constant comment that the solutions are not descriptive and technical, but attitudinal and ethical. We must achieve a new consciousness, it is claimed, before our old ways destroy us. The task, for example, is not to find some intermediate method of reducing the amount of mercury seeping into the oceans. Emergency measures will only briefly forestall the impending catastrophe. What is needed, it is claimed, is a repentance, a conversion, a revolutionized commitment to a new lifestyle. This is the rhetoric of apocalyptic. Only a renewed ethical consciousness that prompts zealous personal and political action can save us now. The intertwined complexity of the problem will not be met by some piecemeal solution. Let us attempt to extract the ethical derivatives of the apocalyptic consciousness and establish evaluative principles for the problems we shall subsequently discuss.

As we study the development of apocalyptic consciousness, we find the following elements. First there exists a conviction that present natural and historical (political) crises are but the advent of a greater struggle in which the judgments of God will be vividly portrayed. This view of cosmic travail is accompanied by a messianic hope (the expectance of deliverance), a coming judgment, punishment of the wicked, eradication of evil, and the establishment of good. At the height of the consciousness is an ecstatic vision of a golden age, a completely new order where the righteous reign with God. This travail is superseded by the arrival of a new heaven and a new earth.

Apocalyptic consciousness develops when the present situation is one of tribulation, because all things groan in the travail, that the new may be born. The contemporary situation has those qualities. Oppression and injustice are politically condoned and technologically implemented. Genocide is rampant. The Western attitude might be called a barricading or covered-wagon posture. When the outsiders attack, the wagons pull into a tight circle to protect the life and goods inside. As the underdeveloped nations strive for an equitable share of the earth's resources and full participation in world markets, and as the environment howls at the plunder we have made in the world, our first reaction is to withdraw into a self-protective stance. Forcefully tube-feeding a dying person, while across the world children die of starvation is an apocalyptic scenario.

The truth about our time is that a comfortable, establishmentarian mentality exists side by side with a seething apocalyptic mentality. The one reason for hope is that the protectionists are beginning to see that they are wrong, that affluence built on the labor and sacrifice of others and the manipulation of markets is ultimately inimical to self-interest. This attitude of satisfaction is antagonistic to the apocalyptic. The mentality rationalizes injustice and shrinks from the impending crisis. It often seeks satisfaction in the present physical moments, for "tomorrow we die." "A very common attitude of flight is entrenchment in the present," writes Polak. "Then from moment to moment, one can find certainty and also enjoy the fulfillment in pleasure (*carpe diem*). The future (hoped for or feared) does not enter into consideration; it is eliminated with a stroke of the pen." [22]

The apocalyptic consciousness surfaces in culture during "times of trouble." During periods of order and peace, it remains submerged in the collective subconscious. The rationalistic and idealistic epochis of Western history are periods when apocalyptic yields to prognosis, prophecy to planning, and divine providence to human vision. Yet in times of over-rationalization like ours, the dimensions of mystery and depth are recovered by a revival of apocalyptic. Indeed, it might be argued that the urgent efforts to plan future technological development in an ethical way reflect, in a secular fashion, the predictive side of apocalyptic expectation. Newton, Hegel, and Edwards, men of scientific learning, were intensely interested in the eschatological schemata of events in the apocalypse. Newton felt so strongly that a wholistic view of nature depended upon the joining of rationalistic and apocalyptic insight that after 1692, he devoted his entire life to the study of prophecy. Today we witness a generation of young people—scientists and engineers, soundly schooled in the scientific method—turning to astrology, mysticism, and apocalyptic to discover the lost vistas and dimensions of life. In *Birth Ethics* (Crossroad, 1989) and *Death Ethics* (Trinity, 1992), I have argued that apocalyptic consciousness is an integral biological and developmental dimension of human conscience.

Pertinent to our thesis is the way the worldview is related to action and apocalyptic is related to prophecy and ethics. A mentality of discontent combined with an intense creativity is engendered by apocalyptic. That creativity can be expressed constructively or destructively. The prophet exercised the twofold function of forth-telling and pretelling. Forth-telling is prompted by the discontent ethic of apocalyptic consciousness. Because of the splendor of God's coming Kingdom and the desperate injustice of the present situation, a strong voice of protest and anger is raised. Prophetic consciousness, in this sense, sees through the present. It discerns the moral compromise, then speaks the word and enacts the deed of truth. In the period of the kings, Elijah saw through the misdirected loyalties of God's people and the concomitant personal and social evils. Amos perceived the seeds of destruction in eighth-century Israel. He warned the people, indicating the lingering possibility of repentance and correction, then finally affirmed the enduring grace, return, and justice of God.

The predictive element of prophecy is perhaps stronger in apocalyptic consciousness. Here the vision perceives the future in an ethical sense. Since history is the arena where God discloses God's purpose, present trends can be extrapolated into the future. The vindication of God can be read back into the present. Daniel interprets the Babylonian king's dream as a disclosure of both present political degeneration and its future consequences (Daniel 2). Ezekiel anticipates a coming invasion from an unstable present state of affairs (Ezekiel 38–39). At the heart of biblical prophecy and apocalyptic, the vision of justice comes not from crystal-ball gazing, but rather from honest ethical discernment of the present, in the light of the kingly justice of God.

"Ethics," says Amos Wilder, "was inextricably implied in the best apocalyptic; it was assumed. The eschatological hope was only for the righteous." [23] So intense was the ethical quality of late Jewish apocalyptic that it leads to a radical justificationism, pharisaism, moral pride, and exclusivism in the Qumran communities. The mentality either evoked a radical political activism (Maccabees) or an intense ascetic withdrawal and waiting (Essenes). "Apocalyptic," writes W. D. Davies, "was the outcome of a profound ethical seriousness which was no less concerned with the observance of the Torah than was Pharisaism." [24]

Two ethical principles are anchored in this consciousness. The creativity principle affirms that history is recaptured within the will of God. Therefore: (a) the earth is not a degenerative process, but rather stands at the threshold of regeneration and redemption; the negative principle at the other pole of the dialectic affirms, with critical discontented spirit that (b) the Kingdom will be fashioned by God. Ultimately, it is not a work of humankind. These principles bear on all features of the technological project in general and the biomedical project in particular. All subprojects such as the eugenic (genome project), ephenic (transplantation, rebuilding bodies with machines), and euthanasic (technologically engineered death) can be assessed by this couplet of principles.

(a) For centuries now, the second law of thermodynamics has had the same effect on scientific optimism that apocalyptic has had on religious hope. Both intuitive sensations sense that the earth will not be here forever. All of nature's molecules are in the process of rearrangement to more and more randomness. All heat that is released through the energy conversion process eventually dissipates itself and cannot be recovered. Entropy has been regarded, rightly or wrongly, as a "wearing down process." At best, it is a process by which nothing new is added. Add to this the astonishingly recent discovery that the earth is finite, with a shallow envelope of air and water sustaining its life, and you have a mentality that sees nature caught up in an inevitable process of degeneration. Evolutionary theory adds to this long-range pessimism regarding the future of human life on the earth. Humans, it is claimed, will eventually go the way of all species as we are ground under in the selection process. In cosmic terms, this small speck we call earth also has a most tenuous prospect in the vast universe. That this singular species would survive, amid the proliferative loss of existent species on this planet so close to being rendered lifeless by excessive heat or cold, or some collision in this expanding and contracting universe, may be an expression of unrealistic audacity. On the other hand, that these beings called human have evolved during more than four million years on a planet with a multibillion-year geologic history is a miracle engendering gratitude and resolute future purpose.

Philosophers of history such as Spengler see human affairs controlled by the same forces of growth, maturation, and decay that control the plants and the seasons. Historian Bertrand Russell writes:

> The same laws which produce growth also produce decay. Some day, the sun will grow cold, and life on the earth will cease. The whole epoch of animals and plants is only an interlude between ages that were too hot and ages that will be too cold. There is no law of cosmic progress, but only an oscillation upward and downward, with a slow trend downward on the balance swing to the diffusion of energy.... From evolution ... no ultimately optimistic philosophy can be validly inferred.[25]

Expounding this viewpoint with apocalyptic alarm are many groups of environmentalists today. They rightly locate our culture's contemptuous misuse of the environment and warn of impending catastrophe if we persist in our ways. At their best, they call for heightened responsibility and immediate reversal of the damaging activity. More frequently, unfortunately, they see our civilization caught up in an irreversible process of degradation. Inherent, and thought to be inevitable, human avarice and greed is internationalized in the puritan-capitalist ethic. The global political power structures have no possibility of concerted action to remedy the situation. Civilization, it is argued, is a rapid process of incipient doom. In the words of shunned jurist Robert Bork, we are "slouching toward Gomorrah."

A contrasting position is forwarded by a group that might be called the "negantropists." These scientists and humanists contend that a reverse process is going on, whereby humankind is gathering energy into its control and rapidly bringing a process of increasing order around the nexus of the human mind and control. Chief advocates of this position include Teihard de Chardin and Buckminster Fuller. They contend that vast creativity inheres in the human enterprise. This creativity not only has the prospect of warding off the deleterious aspects of entropy and evolution, but of building up through humanity an ideal world, where capacities are enlarged, societies enriched, and relationships with environment renewed toward qualitative excellence.

The optimism and creativity of these positions, as well as all those who hold out intense hope against what appears to be inevitable disaster, are truly children of the apocalypticists. They dream of the Kingdom coming as they long for the rupture wherein the will of God will be disclosed, and God's golden age will be ushered in.

In the earlier Hebrew apocalyptic, we see the roots of this consciousness. Zechariah (1–8), for example, envisions a great conflagration, through which will emerge a faithful people in a goodly land, where "the vine shall give fruit and the ground shall give increase" (8:12). The messianic leader (Zechariah 3:8; Micah 5:3ff.; Isaiah 11:1; Jeremiah 23:5ff.) will rise up to restore the goodness of God's creation, even though the great judgment expressed is coming (Isaiah 24–27) in cosmic catastrophe. An age is coming when no child will die too soon nor any adult fail to live out his or her life (Isaiah 65). This will be but the prelude to the establishment of God's perfect will in the creation.

The first ethical axiom of apocalyptic consciousness, rooted in our early religious traditions, mediated through Judaic-Christian heritage, contends that vibrant hope in the impending kingdom of God repudiates any idea of a degenerating cosmos and ultimate nihilism. Rather than resigning ourselves to cruel fate, we creatively work in this hope to achieve that Kingdom. We know it is God's gift, not our accomplishment. We are instruments to bring about its fulfillment. Moltmann writes:

> Where such a hope comes to life, suffering from the unfulfilled and unfree aspects of life develops. It is not only a suffering from earthly anguish but, even more, a suffering from the anguish of the world, the whole "eagerly awaiting creation," which is expressed, revealed, and incorporated in the resurrected hope.[26]

This creative side of the apocalyptic consciousness prompts humans to build the earth, to exercise hope in planning, working always under the moral scrutiny of a divine Justice. It has a quality of waiting and patience, as well as a willingness to bear the suffering that righteous creativity entails. Ultimately, humans trust in God to establish God's good order of things, acknowledging the ultimate limitation of their noblest efforts and accomplishments.

(b) The other pole of apocalyptic ethical consciousness is one of discontent. It affirms the final relativity of all human action, the propensity to idolatry in all human accomplishment, and the ultimate acknowledgment that the Kingdom is not humankind's autonomous project. Apocalyptic ethics inspire the Kingdom and the *shalom* of justice while they discount utopia. The abiding message of apocalyptic, writes Rowley, is that "our ideal schemes may strike against many hard and grim realities and be torn to shreds. . . . We forget that 'a person's life consisteth not in the abundance of the things which he/she posesseth' (Luke 12:15)."[27]

Humanity sensitized with apocalyptic awareness reminds us of the frailty of our present systems and structures. Hope, contends Ernst Bloch, is a vision of the Kingdom, in the light of which all else appears penultimate and corrupt, therefore arousing our anger and discontent. Humans possessed with such vision long for a new and different situation. We therefore marshall energy and activity to the tasks of transformation. We must acknowledge at this point that for the time being, although often averse to freedom, Marxists had seized the essence of apocalyptic ethics and gained the initiative in fashioning the new world. Today, as Marxism disappears in world history, political systems of freedom flourish, accenting liberty often at the neglect of justice and community. The weakness of the collectivist system, of course, was that it did not bring to bear principles of judgment and discontent on its own works. Economic and technical schemes in the system often begin to carry an unimpeachable beaurocratic and totalitarian character. Bloch shows that although the biblical Kingdom always remains in the future, it is the temporal rupture, not a pietistic otherworldly utopia. With the seers of apocalyptic vision, Bloch affirms that discontent prompts us to build the kingdom of love, stimulated by the hope for its temporal and secular advent.

Much indebted to Bloch, Moltmann shows how a "permanent iconoclasm" proceeds from this apocalyptic hope. "It is the motor, the mainspring, the torture of history, for it points out the perennial incompleteness of that which has become and that which is becoming in the reality desired and sought for in hope."[28] Suffering and discontent indeed spur the remedial and creative actions that pursue the Kingdom. "It is the suffering from the earthly anguish and unfree human conditions . . . that wishes happiness for the poor and freedom for the humiliated and is, therefore, ready to make investments."[29]

Although humans propose new actions to alleviate what is wrong and bring about some semblance of that state of affairs that we apocalyptically envision, we always remember that even our best proposals become infected with the same corrupt motives that invalidated the former schemes. We recall that our function, under God, is not to assume, as the apocalypticists did and do, that evil must be eradicated by doing away with the "unrighteous." Our human task is rather to establish justice and leave judgment to God. The horsemen of the apocalypse (Revelation 6) are a specter of forces in the world to be challenged in our care for the earth: hunger, diseases, war. The apocalypticists, in distortion of their vision, saw as their task the sweeping away of evil people, the unrighteous. Even if we faithfully leave this to some messiah-warrior whom we only follow, we are at fault for seeking to rupture the divine pattern and schedule of Kingdom actualization with our own frantic desires.

> The apocalypticists did not for a moment imagine that the Kingdom of God would be established by human means. It could be established only by a divine act. It would be a stone cut without hands that would become a mountain, or one like unto a Son of Man coming on the clouds of heaven.[30]

We might conclude this section establishing the two axioms with a reference to the apocalyptic vision of humanity. D. S. Russell, in a careful analysis of the apocalyptic consciousness, shows that "in Israelite thought humankind is conceived, not so much in dual fashion as 'body' and 'soul,' but synthetically as a unit of vital power (in current terminology), a psychophysical organism."[31]

Paul Ramsey contrasts this view with what he calls "the genetic apocalypse." This scientific alarmism, expounded by H. J. Muller and others, argues that a deleterious gene load is building up in the pool, and raw natural process will be left no alternative but a devastating climax, since humankind has successfully subverted natural selection. Muller, of course, calls for eugenic proposals (sperm banks), since nature's wisdom has been apocalyticized by harmful human transformations. Since we have so severely compromised the future, we must now assume rigorous control, the norms of which will be humanly conceived excellence. The broad contours of the search for life and health in modern society are animated by the good hope and threatened by the violent dread of apocalyptic conscience.

In contrast to this burdensome hope, faithful people, says Ramsey, meet the world expecting another apocalypse, another eschaton:

> Anyone who intends the world as a Jew or as a Christian . . . goes forth to meet the collision of planets or the running down of suns, and he/she exists toward a future that may contain a genetic apocalypse with his/her eye fixed on another eschaton. . . . (I believe with unswerving faith in the coming of the Messiah).[32]

In the biblical apocalyptic view, humans not only possess psychological and physical nature but also are spiritual beings. As we ponder and plan the human future, we must view it as God's future. We will be wise to heed the apocalyptic counsel that humans are the vessels and instruments of God. Our scientific schemes to transform humanity should remain modest and not rupture that deeper design and plan. Many leading scientists have expressed this caution in publications.[33]

Apocalyptic consciousness, with its derivative values, is necessary for our turbulent times. It hears the sense of urgency, the strong vision of Kingdom, the humble estimate of humanity needed today. Yet apocalyptic also fashions the gentle wisdom of Christian hope in the history of our consciousness. Although apocalyptic shapes and influences the beginnings of Christianity, another ethic, equally urgent in expectation of the Kingdom but more faithful in waiting, planning, and living responsibly for the long vistas of history, awaits to be born. It is to this transformation of Greek, Hebrew, and apocalyptic consciousness in its prac-

tical aspects that we now turn. Here human conscience is transmuted beyond the blissful immediacy of the animals.

> Thou art blest compar'd wi' me!
> The present only toucheth Thee.
> But oh! I backward cast my e'e
>   on prospects dear!
> an' forward tho' I canna see,
>   I guess an' fear!
>
> *Robert Burns, "To a Mouse"*
> *(Startled while plowing a field)*

Symbols of Desired Utopia

An energy and hope, a discontent and desire, is found in human
ethical consciousness, in part the result of our theological history, in
part the natural outgrowth of inquiring and improving human mentality. In our discussion of Christian consciousness of the future and
the kingdom of God, we noted the various ways in which human
imagination perceives a desired future. Human hopes are sometimes
transcendentally located, sustaining a vision and informing a critique
of the present. At other times, attempts are made to bring images of
hope and desired utopia into present actualization. We seek to form
communities that anticipate and precipitate the vision. In most
instances, however, there is a blending of these two understandings.
In medicine today, for example, the attempt is made to bring the
vision of a completely healthy society and individual as near approximation as possible. Depending upon the intensity of the hope
symbol, the healthy individual may be defined as one physically
immortal, disease-immune, or merely capable of coping. The clini-
cal-therapeutic results that most resembles that vision becomes the
practical objective. In such cases, we deal as much with "archetypal
desires" (Gabor) as desires rooted in ultimate hope. The hope
vision, in other words, is combined with a practical realism. In this
attitude, discontent does not collapse into despair, because hope is
sustained in growth and advance toward the goal.

Symbols of desired *utopias* (no places) or *topias* (places) concern
themselves generally with the whole of life. Health, happiness,

conviviality, all the objectives of fulfillment, are usually encom-
passed in the vision. In this section, I will seek to show how hope
symbols, rooted in fundamental moral and technical consciousness of religious eschatology, form concrete ethical principles. As
with cognate apocalyptic values, hope principles engender discontent and rejection of a present situation and sustain the quest for a
desired situation.

We have noted that Christianity emerged in the Greek world
during the Roman Empire. Its emergence was shaped in the cru-
cible of Jewish apocalyptic and its ethic. The followers of Jesus are
cautioned not to predict the times or seasons of God's action, but
rather to read "the signs of the times" and be ready for that
advent. They are discouraged from holy war and violence. Even
the eruption of miracles and healings are to be greeted with a
peculiar reticence, even silence.

Whether it was disappointment at the delay of *Parousia* or gradual establishment of the Apostolic Church and Petrine Christianity, the New Testament ethic abandons the urgency and passion of
apocalyptic. The new ethos is characterized by a *parenesis* that
faithfully waits, rigorously works, and teaches and disciplines and
lovingly shapes its life and orders. This new social consciousness
envisions a long future on God's good earth; it develops a long-
range hope. The love ethic, the ethic of care, becomes the un-
comfortable mandate of the Christian community.

Each time our consciousness and conscience symbolize a
desired world, it prompts the response of care in our active life.
This can be taking care of oneself or caring for another. The
highest purpose in human life is to care for another. This is the
prime principle of ethical hope.

Hope and Care

There is no deeper meaning to human existence. A passion for
God is empty without a passion for human good. Hope that does
not issue in care is illusion. When humans care, they are good,
they *act* well, they are human. Eric Erickson has shown how
responsible maturity entails the capacity to love with care. The

religious and ethical quality of a person who cares or one who doesn't care is not ultimately determined by the effect. Faulkner's idiot Benjy can care for his sister Caddie, and it is good, however ineffectual. Where there is a choice, care that helps is to be desired. So technical capacity becomes part of humankind's care. Technology is the extension of our being and action. The things we make enable us to care with effect. Here technology is swept into the sphere of value. Today, through knowledge, power, and technique, humankind is achieving the capacity to care effectively. We can see pain and do something about it.

Care is rooted in human existence as a hoping being. Interpreting Heidegger's *Being and Time,* Schubert Ogden notes that "precisely as care, human existence has a relation not only to the being of others, but also to itself: to its past through memory . . . to its own future possibilities by anticipation."[34] Human care for the world is part of our self-care for others. When I see thirty children along the ship channel hospitalized from mercury poisoning, I must go to the chemical plants whose effluents constitute the problem's etiology. When dozens of unexpected deaths occur in a neighborhood near a dump, we try to go to the source. When high proportions of births in the inner city are premature or otherwise high-risk, we ask why and seek to ameliorate the condition. We may even go beyond to the social-political basis of that technical problem.

The disciplines of care have traditionally sustained ethical vision and guided moral choice. We stand today at the dawn of a new age, when our civilization must declare its convictions about the destiny of human life. How we are going to exercise our power over the course of human life? Despite our discomfort, we are being forced to declare what we believe to be ontologically and ethically normative about persons and how we shall act on that commitment.

To ask what is normatively human is to invite a commitment. Here we declare that we will take our stand with persons and the human community. Here we affirm that we will stand before persons as advocates to safeguard them from assault. This commitment then directs action. Positively, it involves the responsible transmission of life to a new generation. It also involves nurturing to fullest potential those lives already entrusted to our care. Negatively, this commitment checks our propensity to destroy and disregard those lives already within our care.

We owe to those persons we have received into the human community nothing less than the secular equivalent of Luther's claim on the church. He said that a child is truly saved when the congregation means its baptism. To generate and receive new life into the human community is a blessed gift and an awesome responsibility. As we evaluate the nature of human life and our power over that life, I invite you to consider several illustrative cases at the inception of life—procreation, abortion, genetic medicine—what we might call perinatal or nativity ethics. This realm of case study will set the stage for the final section of the book, in which we apply the ethical system we have developed to concrete issues of life and health.

Let me acknowledge my bias at the outset. My work in medical ethics across the years has sought to derive secular values from evangelical Christian ethics. I am a student of Helmut Thielicke, the greatest theological ethicist of our time. Though you will sense Thielickean themes in my work, I differ from him in one important way. I am not content merely to do ethics for the Christian community alone, as Thielicke and Paul Lehmann, for example, have done so eloquently. I am foolhardy enough and sufficiently corrupted by the great translators of religious theory into secular practice, Paul Ramsey, James Gustafson, and Joe Fletcher, to seek from these faith-based systems viable ethical doctrine for our pluralistic and humanistic society.

Summary

The guiding and enduring values of Judeo-Christian faith have shaped our culture in all its manifestations, especially in the quest for well-being, health, cure of disease, and avoidance of death. We have found positive and negative values in the basic ethical structure of the Decalogue. A partial tableau of these values can be summarized.

Do

- heal the sick
- prevent disease
- prolong life
- repair and replace failing functions
- enhance genetic endowment

Do Not

- *do not kill*
- *do not harm*
- *do not cause suffering*
- *do not prolong dying*
- *do not cause environmental (toxic) damage*

The impulses and restraints we have found in our composite heritage of belief and ethics constitute an ethos that we can now explore in the specific projects and programs that seek and serve well-being.

— CHAPTER FOUR —

The Pursuit of Happiness and the Vision of Health

The exploration that we propose in this book must begin with the question of who we are as a people and where we are going in our search for life and health. This question focuses and interrelates concerns of medicine, politics, and religion. I use the wonderful old word religiomedici to designate this grand enterprise. The worldwide perception that health and good life are possible amid the morbidities of existence is intensely sharpened in the Western culture, and especially in the cultural legacy of pluralism. Our story therefore begins in the American version of that cultural ethos. The imagination that founded the American nation is one of the most compelling visions ever to capture the minds and hearts of people. In many ways, the mid-eighteenth century in the colonies was one of those rare moments when philosophers were kings.

At the heart of that founding imagination which has endured for more than two centuries is a human quality that Thomas Jefferson called "the pursuit of happiness." He has transposed John Locke's right to property into a more subtle guarantor of human well-being—still worldly and material—but now refined from the dross of feudal fatalism, with its inheritance customs and the endemic exploitation of early capitalism. Now happiness is a right of every person, great and small. The phrase "the pursuit of happiness" runs back through the myriad roots of Jefferson's learning: The Enlightenment, Calvanistic Puritanism, the Romanticism of the philosophs. The "pursuit of happiness," along with life and liberty, was a perfect right, a natural endowment, a divine investiture, intrinsic to humans as persons—inalienable and inviolable. Government has as its principal task to see that no powers snatch this right from the people; a secondary task is to provide the salience—the atmosphere of equality and justice—within which the pursuit of happiness is nurtured. Freedom, for well-being, for all, from God, is close to the cardinal tenet of the American creed.

Today, as we search for the deeper roots and farthest branches of our national destiny in the health science project, we find a vision of well-being, a pursuit of happiness, a quest for life and health that, rightly sought, is the glory, and wrongly sought is the tragedy of our nation. It is glory, in that it provides both substance and energy to our hopes in the realm of health and disease. It is a danger, should we fail to temper our expectations in accord with fundamental justice and sensibility, which is an integral part of that inherited vision. We now see how the inherent values we have just reviewed rightly chasten our ambitious projects.

Let us explore the following thesis: As we pursue happiness and (as part of that pursuit) formulate a national health agenda, let us look back and recover the simple justice of our biblical heritage, that our hope for well-being can be cleansed from illusion and injustice, and our national destiny be refined. This simple justice, announced from the mists of prehistory in what became the Decalogue, affirmed by the eighth-century Hebrew prophets, is charted in most radical form in Jesus' Sermon on the Mount. This text was deeply formative as Jefferson was writing the Declaration and Madison and others were drafting the Constitution. Its simple wisdom will serve us well as we reflect upon a health policy with both its research agenda and its delivery system.

Let us first observe the way the "pursuit of happiness" notion develops in political philosophy and comes to shape modern biomedical policy. Second, we will confront realities of the economies of life on the one hand and the simple wisdom of prophetic justice on the other, which together lead us to temper, contour, and redirect this pursuit. In the light of this, we finally can sketch a realistic vision of well-being, an attainable goal for a health system that can be translated into a viable commitment to health-care policy to better serve the happiness of the human family.

The Development of the Idea of Pursuit of Happiness

Thomas Jefferson is the American Enlightenment. President John Kennedy, hosting a group of Nobel Prize winners, described his guests as the "most extraordinary collection of talent . . . that has ever been gathered together at the White House—with the possible exception of when Thomas Jefferson dined alone."[1] If anything, we have here an understatement; historian, scientist, philosopher, architect, Jefferson was most of all the advocate of the rights of humankind and the responsibility of government to protect and achieve these rights.

The two primary sources of Jefferson's worldview—the Enlightenment philosophers and the covenantal theologians—believed with Hebraic Exodus faith that intrinsic to human freedom was the right to survive, to be healthy and happy. The most fundamental of human rights was the right to life and health. This optimism is all the more remarkable, since this is still, according to William McNeill's great study, "The Age of the Plagues."[2] Real happiness, said a French marquis, consists in not having any crime on the conscience, being able to rest content in the station to which God has called us and, finally, receiving a clean bill of health. That's an eighteenth-century way of saying, "If you've got your health, you've got just about everything."[3]

The right to happiness is rooted in nature and nature's God. A direct line of influence can be traced from primitive wisdom, Hebraic and Greek tradition to Boethius, then to Aquinas and Calvin. From Calvin, it moves to the French and Scottish philosophers and the English Puritans, to John Locke, to John Witherspoon, to Madison, Jefferson, and the other Constitutional fathers. Madison and Adams had a little more of Calvin's stern serenity than did Jefferson, who was delightfully apostate. But on the issue of happiness, they were in perfect accord. "Man is the glory of God," wrote Calvin. "The chief purpose of man is to glorify God and enjoy him forever," wrote the Westminster Divines under Cromwell's protectorate.

John Locke was raised by his Puritan father in the shadow of the Westminster assemblies. He absorbed the thought of the Puritan Divines. These beliefs were in the air at the time: toleration; the exploitative tendencies of humans; the noble justice of the civil contract within the divine covenant; the essential goodness and legitimacy of the search for well-being here and now; the theme of stewardship—of the body, of marriage, of the polis. The approximation of rights of the people under God here on earth was the human task. Locke taught Jefferson; Witherspoon taught Madison, along with twelve other members of the Continental Congress who assembled in Philadelphia in that epochal convention. Madison spent a year after his graduation from Princeton studying the Bible in Greek and Hebrew, as well as the constitutions of predecessor states, all under the tutelage of the Scots-Presbyterian pastor, president John Witherspoon.

Though steeped in this same tradition, Jefferson is an innovator:

> We hold these truths to be self-evident, that all men are created equal, that they are endowed by their Creator with certain unalienable Rights, that among these are Life, Liberty and the pursuit of Happiness.

Jefferson wrote the majestic second paragraph of the Declaration of Independence while pining away for his young bride, cooped up in the second floor of the Graff house, with the added irritant of Adams and Franklin pacing nervously outside. The Declaration goes on:

> That Whenever any Form of Government becomes destructive of these ends, it is the Right of the People to alter or to abolish it, and to institute new Government, laying its foundation on such principles and organizing its powers in such form, as to them shall seem most likely to effect their Safety and Happiness.

Safety and survival are preliminary to quality life. Health is not much good without security; D.O.D. and H.H.S. are our poor efforts to be true to Jefferson. But we must be most careful not to confuse safety with happiness, security with health, bread with salvation. In clinical medicine, we know that often, preservation of life, alleviation of suffering, and achievement of health are often values in conflict. Life is the necessary substratum of health. Health is a substratum upon which happiness can be built. It is neither necessary nor sufficient cause, but it surely helps.

That happiness has physical and spiritual roots is a common assumption in our culture. "Upon this all speculative philosophers will agree," wrote John Adams in 1776, "that the happiness of society is the end of government, as all divines and moral philosophers will agree that happiness of the individual is the end of man."[4] The blending of Calvin and Rousseau, of Locke and Roger Williams, is felt in all the Constitutional fathers.

The secular and transcending loci of happiness were emphasized in both the rational and the religious Enlightenment, called respectively the *Aufklarung* and the Great Awakening. The secular Enlightenment saw human ills as caused by bad institutions. The Calvinistic Enlightenment saw moral failure in the heart and will of humankind as the root of malignancy and unhappiness. For the former, science and education hold the key to happiness; for the latter, justice and moral regeneration hold the key. Now these blend into a cultural synthesis. Happiness is possible here and now, with reason, good politics, and sound institutions, said the philosophs. Felicity is to be found in this life and beyond, said the Christians. Blending these sentiments in the first Inaugural Address in 1801, Jefferson invoked "the blessings of providence, which by all its dispensations proves that it delights in the happiness of man here and the greater happiness hereafter."[5]

But humans are never content with the uncertainty of eternal bliss. We seek signs here and now. Invoking the primal myth that disease and death entered the world because of some wrong in humanity, we search for ways to right that wrong. We now look for signs of physical healing in the Creation as witness to redemption overcoming the cosmic fall. The search for happiness transmutes into an almost purely material quest. Interestingly, the materialization process begins with a religious impulse, corroborating perhaps the accusation that Western religions are secular at heart.

The important spiritual prelude to the Constitutional Convention was the Great Awakening. Jonathan Edwards saw two public health events as signals of Kingdom come, of millennium. First, drunkards were being reformed under the influence of the first public-health agency, the temperance movement. Second, inoculation was working against smallpox, or so it appeared. Edwards trusted his mentor Cotton Mather, the greatest religious and scientific thinker of his time, as he inoculated his own children. Edwards had himself inoculated as an encouragement to the citizens of Princeton, where he had become university president (regrettably, the exemplar guinea pig died).

The Calvinistic Puritans, whose grandchildren were to found this nation, felt that the end times would be marked by signs in the physical realm—the end of war, of intemperance, of plagues, of slaveholding. Today, although we see millennium as human task as much as divine gift, the yearnings for physical happiness are the same. The night is far spent; the messianic dawn is near. The pursuit of happiness is now embodied in our biomedical agenda.

Material well-being had always been part of the pursuit of happiness, especially in the Enlightenment. Henry Steele Commager, in his masterful studies of the period, identifies the content of the idea of progress toward happiness in the eighteenth century.

> The American conception of progress was not a matter of cultural refinement but of material welfare and of freedom, a matter of health, wealth and education. . . . It was—and long remained—a matter of milk for the children, meat on the table, a well-built

house and a well-filled woodshed. Cattle and sheep in the pastures and hay in the barn.[6]

As worldly satisfactions and securities increase, the terrors of nature and survival diminish and a new quality of inner terror is born. Stripped of heaven by the *Religionskritik* of Marx and Freud, humans, in both anxiety and aspiration, begin to ask a new question, the inversion of the old one: "Is there life—abundant life— before death?" The modern age is not even as certain as Jefferson about the hereafter. The ebbtide of the sea of faith has departed from the shores of human life. Nietzsche, whose Monticello was in and around the Swiss Alps, heard not Jefferson's harmonious song, but a plaintive cry from nature:

> Whither does the earth now move?
> Wither do we move? Away from all suns?
> Backward, sideways, forward, in all directions?
> Is there still an above or below?
> Do we not stray as through infinite nothingness?
> Does not empty space breathe upon us?

As the sense of divine providence in and through nature constricts, and both self-sufficiency and anxiety enlarge, humanity chooses the tragicomic option of apotheosis—self-deification.

"If gods are no more in the earth," jested Schubert in *Die Winterreise*, "then we ourselves are gods." In a more somber mood, Dag Hammarskjöld weighed the new burden: "Through the ages we have thought that we must be responsible to God; now we must be responsible for God."[7] "Here on Earth," said John Kennedy, "God's work must truly be our own." In that same inaugural, he said:

> We are called to bear the burden of a long twilight struggle, year in and year out, rejoicing in hope, patient in tribulation—a struggle against the common enemies of humanity: tyranny, poverty, disease, and war itself.[8]

Disease and death, once the demonic scourge or the inscrutable divine quarantines, must now be grasped by human science and attacked with technology.

Optimistically, the pursuit persisted. On the eve of the First World War, when Karl Barth and Martin Heidegger had already shattered the illusion of Enlightenment optimism, when technology was about to unleash devastation heretofore unknown to humankind, Sir William Osler exuded:

> To have lived through an epoch, matched only by two in the story of the race, to have shared in its long struggle, to have witnessed its final victory—to have done this has been a wonderful privilege. To have outgrown age-old theories of humanity and nature, to have seen west separated from east in the tangled skein of human thought, to have lived in a world remaking, these are among the thrills and triumphs of the Victorian of my generation. To a childhood and youth came echoes of the controversy that Aristarchus began, Copernicus continued, and Darwin ended, that put the microcosm in line with the microcosm, and for the golden age of Eden substituted the *tellus dura* of Lucretius. Think of the Cimmerian darkness out of which our generation has, at any rate, blazed a path! . . . An age of force followed the final subjugation of nature. The dynamo replaced the steam engine, radiant energy revealed the hidden secrets of matter, to the conquest of the earth was added the control of the air and the mastery of the deep. Nor was it only an age of force. Never before had humans done so much for other humans. The victory over the powers of nature meant also glorious victories of peace, pestilences were checked, the cry of the poor became articulate, and to help the life of the submerged half became the sacred duty of the other. How full we were of the pride of life! In 1910 at Edinburgh, I ended an address on "Human's Redemption of Humanity" with the well-known lines of Shelley, beginning "Happiness and Science dawn though late upon the earth."[9]

Science, yes! The dynamo replaced the Virgin as symbol of human hope in Henry Adams' perception of the 1900 World's Fair. For Norman Mailer, Von Braun's rockets are the shimmering Madonnas of the space age. But the noblest adventures of modern science are launched against infectious disease. The plagues, the destroyers of children, untimely and unnatural deaths, are hunted down and rooted out. Hundreds of World Health Organization officials closed in and eliminated the last remnants of smallpox. Now the sexually transmitted infections and ominous viral diseases such as HIV abound. These, with the idiopathic diseases—the degenerative disorders, metabolic diseases, diseases of the organs, cancer, cardiovascular, and cerebrovascular diseases—are the enemies to be defeated. Today we find ourselves in ambivalence because the cost of the conquest may be greater suffering and unhappiness. We are already tempering our war on disease with certain accommodations. In this day of Dr. Kevorkian, the search for good death becomes the search for good life.

Some years ago the *London Times* reported that 10,000 persons, mostly elderly, expired in city hospitals during the week. In most cases, the cause of death was pneumonia, secondary to influenza. In many cases, antibiotics and vigorous therapies were not used, and one old man's friend was allowed to enter the room and carry the patient away. Conquerable disease was seen as natural and timely in that culture at that time.

Houston is not London. Every two weeks, nine families from Holland journey to the Texas Heart Institute under a program with the Dutch government. That nation had decided that it can afford only two open-heart centers in Utrecht and Amsterdam. Medical priorities did not allow for more extensive facilities to revascularize the heart. Because the morbidity and mortality reduction offered by the heart bypass operation was questionable, and forced into certain priority judgments, that nation decided that crippling angina and death in the fifth, sixth, and seventh decades of life must unfortunately be accepted as natural. In the American culture, perhaps more in Houston than in Philadelphia or Chicago, we have decided that blood-vessel disease, when one is sixty years old, is a problem to be solved by surgery, transplantation, and the artificial heart, and eventually by genetic and lifestyle therapies. To us, such disease has become unnatural, untimely, and unacceptable.

The march goes on. As microorganismic and idiopathic disease diminish, a war is declared on cancer, which Freud called the "last disease." That disease seems to emerge from the roots of our being, when carcinogenic bombardment wears down our defenses.

The knowledge of how cancer works will be like the knowledge of how life itself works. Cancer is life gone wild. The treatments must be anti-life. Methotrexate, for example, is an anti-vitamin. Some now ask: "Can we afford to conquer cancer?" Can we afford the economic costs and the iatrogenic injury—the disease caused by the treatment? A young woman in the M.D. Anderson was treated with 14 grams of Methotrexate—at $14,000 a bottle. Perhaps the head-neck tumor would recede, perhaps even disappear. Perhaps her liver and kidney function would be so damaged by the drug that she would die sooner than if the disease had been allowed to run its natural course. But despite medical heriocs, she lost her life, having offered pioneering courage to the world.

Now we are beginning to push the burden of disease into the realm of mental illness. Apparently there is a constant burden of morbidity that affects humankind. Certainly, morality is a constant. If these assumptions are valid, then biomedical and therapeutic progress are in one sense a misnomer. Alleviating infant mortality is progress, but it has precipitated starvation. Eliminating infections will increase deaths from cancer. Perhaps all we can do is push the burden of disease around on the spectrum. Diminishing morbidity and death from one disease may only increase it in another disease. The therapeutic nihilists, alive and well today as at no time since the Jacksonian era, will ask, Why? Perhaps our progress is only making it necessary for people to suffer in more excruciating, prolonged ways. Some say that we have condemned this generation to suffer chronic debilitating disease. One scientific journal conjectured that the dominant diseases at this century's end will be AIDS and Alzheimer's. There are some developments in our culture which suggest that the final mortality vector, the last disease to conquer, will be suicide. Natural Death Acts, Living Wills, the Oregon Rationing Plan, along with the physician-assisted suicide act and the rapid increase of elective and intended deaths, may express this shift.

Despite these ambivalences, we proceed in the spirit of Goethe's Enlightenment *Faust* in our pursuit of happiness as expressed in the war on disease. The soul will not be damned by inordinate, rational scientific pride—it will be damned by resignation and inaction. So we proceed.

"We can begin to hope," writes Dr. Michael De Bakey, "that disease is not inescapable human destiny. Although death may remain inevitable, it need not occur prematurely or be preceded by acute and protracted suffering." [10] In this prognostication in *The Saturday Review*, he goes on to suggest that all the major chronic disorders will, in the next decades, yield to our control and mastery. "American technology," writes a leading news weekly, "promises to add new dimensions to [our] well-being in times ahead. . . . Ways to cure and prevent most forms of two major killers—cancer and heart disease—are within reach, and creation of life in the test tube should become routine." [11] Add to this the diagnostic and therapeutic yield of the Human Genome project, and a virtual paradise seems near at hand.

Surely disease-free existence will be happiness; or will it? The realization of happiness becomes utopic (no place) in the nineteenth century and dystopic (a bad place) in the twentieth. Although some Dystopias, like Orwell's *Animal Farm*, are political, more are biomedical: *Brave New World, Clockwork Orange, One Flew Over the Cuckoo's Nest.*

To conclude this first point, the modern biomedical quest is the latest transmutation of that ancient cultural yearning that Jefferson called "the pursuit of happiness." It is also the most poignant depth of that quest for well-being, for life and health. Our history is fired with a confidence in progress. Many of us can remember the days before antibiotics. Many can remember the day of childhood diseases, the day of painful dentistry. How rapid our progress seems to be! In hospitals today, it is not at all unusual for patients to hold out hope for cure from some treatment still on the drawing boards or on the bench. And with some justification. Patients with leukemia, Wilms' tumor, Hodgkin's disease, depression caused by lithium deficiency, have been lifted like Lazarus out of the tomb by secrets rushed from the lab by little men in white coats. This experience generates the mentality that it is just a matter of time until we understand this and every disease, and generate its treatment. Every disease, like the muscular degenerative disorders, has its Jerry Lewis and a formidable advocacy constituent. So goes the wonderful yet dangerous wish born in our pursuit of happiness. It is dangerous because we are somewhat uneasy with the powers bequeathed by the realization of our hope.

We must now turn to a moral element in Jefferson's thought to help us resolve the tensions we have recognized.

Contours of the Pursuit: Justice

Jefferson was not only a child of the Enlightenment, he was moved by the bedouin wisdom of Jesus. "To the corruptions of Christianity I am opposed," he said, "but not to the genuine precepts of Jesus himself."[12] The simple, radical justice of Jesus' teachings fascinated and captivated Jefferson. The noncalculating, nondiscriminating goodness of the Nazarene commended his teaching as authentic. It is a deep spring of Jefferson's worldview. In his composition of the Philosophy of Jesus of Nazareth, Jefferson placed in a prominent lace the text that has been called the charter of human happiness, the Beatitudes and its larger context, the Sermon on the Mount.

> Blessed are the poor in spirit, for theirs is the kingdom of heaven;
> Blessed are the meek, for they will inherit the earth.
> (Matthew 5:3, 5 NRSV)

Here is prophetic justice. It is one of the rare points at which the New Testament goes beyond Hebraism. In this profound transvaluation of values, human reason is chastened with a deeper wisdom. In this frame of reference the outcast is embraced; the lowly are exalted; the poor are honored, not despised; the least of these is affirmed. Here are the roots of democracy, of equality, of benevolent disposition toward those who suffer. This holy simplicity, this inversion of material values, was seen by Jefferson as a rational expression of a deeper justice. Like his contemporaries Kant and Hume, his predecessors Erasmus and Cusa, and his successors Tolstoy and Dickens, Jefferson knew that this deeper justice was not sentimentalism but strong prophetic mandate. "I tremble for our nation," he wrote, "when I ponder the fact that God is just. His justice cannot sleep for ever."[13]

Great philosophers, from Plato and Socrates to Aquinas and

Kant, had argued that happiness at root was a moral quality, a matter of living fairly and frugally, not taking more from life than you replenish. For Aristotle, happiness was active life within the purposive norms of nature. Happiness, for all the great philosophers, is simply the ethical life.

Contours of the Pursuit: Economy

Economies of life lead us to the same wisdom as prophetic justice. The reality of living on a finite globe with shortages and limitations has inevitably shaken the religious and political foundations of the American dream. It has cooled the pursuit. We have seen the evidence of the lethal effects of hyperconsumption and hyperacquisitiveness. We have seen again the simple health and happiness known by those who live frugally: the Amish, the Adventists. We have seen that living in a hurry leaves a dull afterglow. Dr. Hans Selye, in his monumental work on stress, has suggested that aging is the expenditure of adaptation energy. "The intelligent way to live," he writes, "is to withdraw (from life's reserve) generously but never expend wastefully." [14] Bernard Shaw expresses the same wisdom in *Doctor's Dilemma:*

> Do not try to live forever. You will not succeed. Use your health even to the point of wearing it out. That is what it is for. Spend all you have before you die; and do not outlive yourself. [15]

Most of our uses of the word *happiness* tend towards the banal. Yet the deep meaning of BEATITUDE is the peaceful expenditure of life in honoring and serving others. When *Psychology Today* asks if the pursuit of happiness is satisfied by sex, money, and drugs, it should know that it is asking the wrong questions. [16] Surely happiness is as much related to love as to sex, to giving as to accumulating, to contemplation as to action.

Our frantic search for material prosperity has left a terrible residue of human suffering and degradation. Our moral task now is to provide inward and outward dimensions to our onward thrust. The good life has been marvelously served by technology. There would be nothing more tragic in this day, when we stand at the threshold of a golden age, when Jefferson's elitist image of material happiness could be made possible for all humankind, than to resign ourselves to technological and therapeutic nihilism. But we must see to it that the earth's wealth is no longer hoarded and inequitably consumed and distributed. We must strive to universally ensure those material bases of happiness: survival, food, shelter, and health.

Part of the problem is the American myth that big is beautiful. I have watched the three great university medical centers in which I have worked build over a billion dollars in new development. We also have from 10 to 40 percent too many beds. It is the genius, but sometimes the stupidity of our nation, to persistently believe that more is better. This mind-set also can be traced to the pioneer Americans. Like a Texas braggart, Jefferson saw greatness in grandeur. In his notes on Virginia, set out during a convalescence (which is a dangerous time for anyone to write), he refutes Count Francois Barbé, who had contended that America's weakness was proved by its failure to provide large physical specimens and a full population. Jefferson convinced the skeptical Count that this was indeed a new paradise, a new promised land. Just weigh the American bear, he wrote, at 410 pounds, against the European—a puny 153. The European beaver is 18 pounds maximum; the American, 40. To finally lay waste to the Count's argument, he had a giant moose tracked down in the wilderness of Maine and shipped to France, there to dwarf the great European deer, just one meter tall. Growth and prosperity must signal goodness; health and longevity surely must signal that this is a chosen people.[17]

But BIG is not necessarily great, as Tom Hanks discovered in the film of that title. Now along comes a Club of Rome, which speaks of limits to growth. Schumacher, an economist, opines that *Small Is Beautiful* (he must be British). Yet the shocks have led to a new sense of life's economy. We must manage our house, our habitat. Living, to be happy, should be simple, frugal, and just. "Walk gently on the earth," cries the Native American. "Kneel in awe before the Spirit of life. Allow the great spirit to receive back your life." "Do not anguish," says the Guru, the stoic; "ameliorate stress into peace."

But hold on! cry the disinherited of our nation and the world. Don't stop now—we have not yet tasted the good life. We built your farms and cities. We want our share of the action. And they cry in our Congress and in the United Nations. We want more energy, more heart-lung machines, more of the goods the earth provides. In Chicago, we have just dismantled one of our great bureaucracies, the public school administration—almost all black. They cry, foul! Their cry is poignant.

In the United States, mortality rates are 80 percent higher for men in families with less than $15,000 income than those with $30,000 plus. Men with fewer than five years of school have mortality rates 64 percent higher than men with a college education. In the cities, the crude death rate is 50 to 100 percent higher among adults and children living in poverty than in middle- and upper-income classes. A black man born in Washington, D.C., can expect eleven fewer years of life than a white man born in Minnesota. Rates for chronic illness show the same socioeconomic variability:

> The prevalence rates per 1,000 persons for arthritis are 297.8 for low-income families vs. 159.8 for upper-income families. For diabetes, 74.1 vs. 30.5. For heart conditions, 138.3 vs. 66.6 For hypertension, 172.7 vs. 105.3. For spine and back impairments, 102.8 vs. 52.2. For loss of teeth, 3 vs. 1.[18]

Senator Humphrey's statement should prompt us to rid ourselves of what my younger son used to call the "nightmirrors" in our dream. "A growing body of research," Humphrey wrote, "shows that fluctuations in unemployment are directly followed by changes in the incidence of mental disorder, homicide, heart and kidney disease, alcoholism, suicide, infant and maternal disorders, and general mortality. That relationship suggests the alarming conclusion that much of our national health and well-being is determined in large degree by economic decisions made in Washington."[19]

The delusion in our hope, the injustice in our action, combined with our native greed, has led us from the layperson's side to abdicate responsibility for health, and from the professional's side to expropriate health care from the people. A most dangerous convergence today, to borrow a quip from Ivan Illich, is found when ravenous consumers and rapacious providers join hands. The solution will be transformation of our hope, accenting justice as concomitant to progress. The pursuit of happiness will require personal, professional, and social transformation. Illich has written:

> The recovery from society-wide iatrogenic disease is a political task. . . . It must be based on grass-roots consensus about the balance between the civil liberty to heal and the civil right to equitable health care.[20]

A Hopeful and Just Vision of Well-Being

Let us sketch the shape of a new, more fitting hope, a more appropriate way to pursue happiness and a derivative health policy. That policy should pursue well-being with vigor, accept death with equanimity, and protect a fair and convivial manner of life among the citizenry. When I speak of health policy, I mean not only the research and delivery aspects, but the right-to-be-born policy, the right-to-be-born-healthy policy, the life-prolongation policy, the right-to-die policy, the medical-triage policy—indeed, the full range of medical ethical issues.

Our active hope for happiness should enliven a science policy that will pursue vigorously the human good now pregnant in biomedical research and practice. We stand at the threshold of numerous breakthroughs of profound significance. New vaccines and biologicals promise to alleviate diseases caused by the virus and other microorganisms. Multiple sclerosis, some forms of diabetes, perhaps some mental diseases caused by neurotropic virus, should soon be understood. Biologicals to enhance immune response and control fertility and conception may also develop. Genetic diagnosis and therapy through counseling, fetal diagnosis, recombinant DNA, and phenotypic therapies hold great promise.

New research on the effects of environment, diets, lifestyles, beliefs, and behaviors on health will make us more capable of ensuring that substratum of physical well-being preliminary to happiness.[21] Organ replacement, improved prosthetics and orthopedics, improved capacities to support and replace human functions (muscular, organ, perhaps even central nervous system functions) with electrical devices—all will enhance the ability of physical medicine to help persons with severe disabilities live more fully.

Multimodel therapies in cancer will increase survival with quality life until the fundamental answers come. Mental illness, arthritis, and other chronic cripplers will enjoy improved curative and management capacity.

While we pioneer these new capacities, we must also alleviate the financial burden with streamlined and multiphasic diagnoses; more accent on preventative health services; more health education and emphasis on self-care; and public financial support, at least for catastrophic illness. It may be necessary to impose upper limits on exotic care, in order to ensure basic nurture for the national, and hopefully the global, population.

This leads to the second point. We need to contour the heroic expressions of our hope and learn to accept death, not only in its mystery and wonder, but in its essential benevolence in the pattern of creation. Hans Jonas has written of "The Burden and Blessing of Mortality." [22] We may need living wills and natural-death acts. Certainly we need public policy stipulates that will protect the medical profession from practicing defensive medicine. In the name of economy, we also must cease destroying the village in order to save it. The operation is not a success if the patient dies, just as the village is not saved if it is destroyed.

Regarding equanimity at this threshold of life, Jefferson again exhibits remarkable wisdom. He wrote to Abigail Adams in 1817:

> The being who presides over this world is essentially benevolent . . . stealing from us one by one, our faculties for enjoyment, searing our sensibilities until satisfied, and fatigued with this leaden interaction, we ask our congé. . . . I heard once a very old friend, who had troubled himself with neither poets nor philosophers, say the same thing in plain prose, that he was tired of pulling off his shoes and stockings at night, and putting them on in the morning. [23]

Although Alex Comfort, author of *The Joy of Sex*, might object to this providential understanding of aging, it is certain that to sustain the tension of happiness we must maintain a healthy dialectic between hope and resignation, clinging to life and laying life down. Seneca speaks wisely in his tract on suicide: "Man should live as long as he should, not as long as he can." Teilhard de Chardin expresses the same delicate equipoise:

> We must struggle against death with all our force, for it is our fundamental destiny as living creatures. But when by virtue of a state of things death takes us, we must experience that paroxysm of faith in life that causes us to abandon ourselves to death as if falling into a greater life.[24]

We need to relearn the ancient grace of conquering disease, debilitation, and death by abiding them with courage, while at the same time working to alleviate them. Some of the deepest moral quandaries known to us accompany the new biomedicine: Accepting known genetic risks, knowingly bringing to birth children with imperfect genetic inheritance, tending newborns with birth defects, approaching life's culmination in death with courage and contentment.

I recently sat with one of my students from the school of public health. He kept vigil in the ICU, where his daughter lay comatose with total brain destruction following an automobile accident. While waiting for a second EEG to confirm death, he called out to her: "Baby, we want you to come back . . . but we know it will hurt. If you're ready to go, it's OK." Hours later, she was disconnected and vitality ceased.

Knowing when to cling to life and when to relinquish it will demand extraordinary wisdom from all of us. To maintain vibrant hope, graceful acceptance, and enduring care in life and death will be one of the great challenges of our time.

When all is said and done, the important breakthroughs in world health and national health care will come from a reassertion of the human perspective. We must find ways to diminish the threat of poisonous environments. We must diminish the external stressors, under-employment, mal-employment, and the malignant over-employment that now devastate our land, where both parents must work in order to achieve their desired levels of affluence and happiness. We must bring back to life the family, the villages, the neighborhoods, even in the midst of the Levittowns of this world. We must reactivate conviviality, imparting life to one another through support, sharing, caring. We need oases of solitude, quiet, deep rest. We need play, exercise, friendly stimulating conversation. Only thus will our present pursuit of happiness, characterized by moods of revenge and "grab all the gusto you can get," ameliorate into gratitude for all that life is.

While writing this chapter, my number-one research associate and book-seller, my mother, provided me with a text that George Washington carried on his person. The poem reflects the tranquility of which we speak:

> These are the things, which once possessed
> will make a life that's truly blessed:
> Round a warm fire, a pleasant joke,
> with chimney ever free from smoke,
> A strength entire, a sparkling bowl,
> A quiet wife, a quiet soul,
> A mind, as well as body whole;
> Prudent simplicity, constant friends,
> A diet which no art commends;
> A merry night without much drinking,
> A happy thought without much thinking.
> Each night by quiet sleep made short;
> A will to be but what thou art.
> Possessed of these, all else defy
> and neither wish nor fear to die.[25]

Life, liberty, and the pursuit of happiness—elusive words. Jefferson left them to future generations to ponder and strive for. Robert Frost meditates on them in his poem "The Black Cottage":

> That's a hard mystery of Jefferson's.
> What did he mean? Of course, the easy way
> is to decide it simply isn't true.
> It might not be. I heard a fellow say so.
> But never mind, the Welshman got it planted
> Where it will trouble us a thousand years.
> Each age will have to reconsider it.[26]

CHAPTER FIVE

Case Studies

Nativity Ethics

To begin, let us picture three cases that challenge to the core our values bearing on the procreation of life. I will consider with you first a conflation of Down syndrome cases. Second, I will sketch the Danville, Illinois, Siamese-twin case, the first I faced when I had moved from Texas to Illinois. Finally, let us ponder the case of a twelve-year-old Oklahoma girl who seeks an abortion. All these are cases that allow us to declare the values and reassert our hope. They are cases in which we see the delicate equipoise of two hope imperatives: where hope in life animates saving power and life sustenance, and conversely, where hope beyond this world sanctions the acceptance of death and the discontinuance of life. These cases evoke the set of imperatives conveyed in our ethical heritage.

In the summer of 1981, our society struggled with three Down syndrome cases. In New York City, a woman pregnant with twins was told that amniocentesis indicated that one fetus had Trisomy 21 (Down syndrome). Responding to the medical options and her physician's counsel, she decided that both lives must be interrupted unless the affected fetus alone could be terminated. This incident provoked many letters, including a series in The New England Journal of Medicine. One physician wrote:

> I am appalled by this gross misuse of medical knowledge by physicians. . . . To destroy a physically affected life because of inconvenience is sufficiently repugnant, but to risk the life of the mother and the life of the normal child brings the practice of medicine to its nadir.

The New York Times (May 8, 1981), quoting from the *Journal* article, continues to note that Dr. Hecht, the writer of the letter, suggested that the mother "had another choice: continuing the pregnancy and permitting the retarded child to be adopted."

The doctors who performed the procedure, Thomas D. Kerenyi and Usha Chitkara, responded that abortion of fetuses found to have genetic abnormalities is an accepted practice.

At roughly the same time, the University of California Medical Center agreed to a $900,000 settlement in a "wrongful life" suit on behalf of a severely retarded baby who might have been aborted if its parents had been told of the availability of this prenatal test. The mother, Maria Aragon, was 37 when she gave birth to the child with Down syndrome. The suit claimed that the hospital had the obligation, given her age, to inform her of the option of amniocentesis.

Finally, a California court relocated custody of a teen-age boy with cardiac stenosis, secondary to Down syndrome, to a family that would permit surgery. The court removed custody from the natural parents, who had claimed that surgery should not be permitted because the child might die on the operating table, or worse yet, might live on to survive them or any member of the family who might care for him.

The Danville Siamese twin case can best be summarized by the following chronology of events:

May 5. 1981:	Siamese twins Jeff and Scott Mueller born at Lakeview Medical Center, Danville, Ill.
May 13:	Vermilion County Circuit Court Judge John P. Meyer placed twins in temporary custody of state and ordered the twins transferred to Children's Memorial Hospital in Chicago, after workers for the Department of Children and Family Services asserted that the infants were being starved to death. DCFS filed juvenile court petition with state's attorney, seeking permanent custody of twins.
May 28:	Vermilion county State's Attorney Edward Litak presented testimony to a grand jury about

the treatment twins received at Lakeview Medical Center, but did not ask for an indictment.

June 5:   At a custody hearing, Judge John P. Meyer upheld the state's contention that the twins had been denied food, water, and medical care, but did not uphold the contention that this had been done at the behest of the parents.

June 7:   Robert Mueller, MD, his wife, Pamela, and Petra Warren, MD, were charged with attempted murder, conspiracy to commit murder, and endangering the life and health of the Muellers' Siamese twin sons. The three appeared before Vermilion County Circuit Court Judge James Robinson and pleaded not guilty to all charges.

June 17:   At a preliminary hearing, Illinois Circuit Court Judge Richard Scott dismissed charges that the Muellers and Dr. Warren had tried to starve infants to death. In dropping the charges of attempted murder against the three, Judge Scott said that there was no probable cause for trying the three. The Siamese twins were surgically separated while under the custody order.

September 17:   Judge John P. Meyer, following recommendations from the Illinois Department of Children and Family Services and the request of the parents, ordered that the Muellers be given physical custody of their twins. The DCFS maintains guardianship.

September 21:   Jeff and Scott Mueller were released from Children's Memorial Hospital in Chicago and returned to their parents in Danville.[1]

September 1986: One child dies after several years in intensive custodial care, suctioned around the clock. The other child is well, attending school. Parents have separated.

The third illustrative case occurred in Oklahoma, a grand land of political paradox. In Oklahoma, we find the seedbed of the moral majority, the Christian right, and also the last frontier of rugged individualism. In sublime irony, Oklahoma City, a haven of conservative thought, on April 19, 1995, became the bombing target of what may have been angry conservative militia-oriented whites. In the early 1980s, Oklahoma was a set-up for the kind of case that inevitably had to come in a day when placards read: "Right to Life," "Life begins at conception," "Withdrawal of public funding for abortion is a crime." The twelve-year-old girl was three months pregnant following a gang rape. The girl's request for an abortion, the fact that she had venereal disease, and the threat that pregnancy posed to her life, prompted the judge to approve the abortion. The girl's mother objected on religious grounds. Her argument contended that if God wanted to terminate the pregnancy, God would induce a miscarriage. With that strange theology in the family, no one was surprised when the girl changed her mind and decided not to have an abortion.

What do these cases have in common? Initially, you might argue that they are exotic, extraordinary cases, which make bad raw material for ethical reflection, just as bad legal cases make bad law. Ethically speaking, though, they are instructive because they are borderline cases. They appear not only at the boundaries of the commonplace, but they also suggest exceptions to common-sense values. An example of a borderline situation was the decision by Bonhoeffer, Thielicke, and others to assassinate Hitler in the July 20, 1944, movement. The proscription of murder had now yielded in the minds of these pastors a mandate to kill this diabolic person. In the same manner, these cases cause us to clarify the parameters of our values and the proper dynamics of our hope.

What core values are at stake in perinatal medicine? They emerge from our composite theological-philanthropical heritage. Initially, we recognize our duty to honor all human lives, even defective lives, as life like ours, life worthy of protection, sacred life. But what happens when foreknowledge exists, so that the birth of a child with Down syndrome, or a monstrous child, or a maliciously conceived child, is a choice and not just an inevitability to accept. Now we are involved in knowledge and complicity in deciding that the birth will take place. Such events no longer can be chalked up to fate or providence; they fall within the realm of our choice and power. Hope and acceptance, freedom and limitation intertwine.

These events that challenge our sense of life affirmation occurred while two strangely contradictory events were transpiring. Starting in the 1980s, it began to become clear that the majority of births in the inner cities of our country were to unmarried mothers. The same year, New York City celebrated the 95th anniversary of the Statue of Liberty.

> Give me your tired, your poor, your huddled masses yearning to breathe free, the wretched refuse of your teeming shore, send these, the homeless, tempest-tossed, to me.

While all were meditating on those powerful words of Emma Lazarus, a handful of bloated blue bodies of shipwrecked Haitians were tossed up on Florida's shores. Boat people seeking proffered liberty and opportunity were washed up on the very shores that invite their exodus from desperate oppression.

We cannot continue the moral inconsistency born in our ambivalent hope. We cannot discountinance abortion, and then have contempt and disregard for the lives we have saved. Hopeful care requires that the moment we create neonatal intensive care units, we also must commit ourselves to create conditions that will allow for the fulfillment of the lives we have salvaged. The lives we have delivered into this world, injured because of prematurity, inherited disease, or intrauterine trauma impose a special responsibility to us. To save swiftly, to then kill slowly, has always been the most despicable form of torture, whether done by medieval kings or Nazi firing squads.

With this opening plea for consistency and commitment, let us now consider three fundamental moral principles that arise in our composite ethical heritage and have a stake in perinatal—indeed in all human—medicine:

- the moral burden of knowledge
- the moral use of freedom
- the moral exercise of power.

Knowledge

Morally conceived, knowledge is a wonderful and terrifying burden. Whether we incline toward the medieval Faust and believe that knowledge leads to damnation, or the Enlightenment version, in which the quest leads to progress and salvation, we cannot deny the biblical vision underlying both of those stories—that knowledge takes us to the gates of hell and heaven. Our knowledge over life and death, with its implied power, is profound: "Deep calls to deep" (Psalm 42:7 NRSV).

Since most of us are Faustian in the Enlightenment sense, we need to remind ourselves of the other side of the equation. To do this, we need to hold our secular ethics up against the raw and brutal rigor of biblical ethics. This, after all, is the moral sense that has given life to our civilization. Jews and Christians have come to know the moral structure of life as a profound struggle between the powers of good and evil, or better, the struggle of God against death in the cosmos. Biblical faith conceives of the world as a contention of those energies of life, healing, and well-being—of God, if you will—with destructive, harmful, diabolic forces, the powers of death. This cosmology is not only the dreadful view of apocalyptic imagination; rather, it is a statement of fact about the essential condition of a human community that has drifted from its moral moorings. Biblical anthropology contends not so much that humankind has overreached, in Promethean fashion, the divine quarantines or limits, but rather that we have shriveled away from our freedom and redeeming responsibility.

We have sublimated our essential nature and destiny, the agapic life of justice, into a disoriented life of malevolence and contempt. In that mutation, we have set loose the powers of chaos in the universe. Loren Eiseley has described vividly the vast chasm of whirling destruction that humans have unleashed into the creation. Today, possessed with this new knowledge: the nuclear secret, the genetic secret, and perhaps now drawing close to the immortality secret, the human race is accelerating the world toward end-time crisis. It may be environmental collapse, nuclear cataclysm, genetic apocalypse, or perhaps some slow and final human degradation, not a bang but a whimper. We are not sure whether God's Noachic or apocalyptic promise will prevail: Will we inherit forgiveness and a new future, or the consummation of human life as we know it?

William Stringfellow has claimed that ethics "concerns human action in relation to the principalities in the Fall, where both human beings and principalities, as well as the rest of creation, exist under the claim that death is morally sovereign in history." [2] Even though human thought and action is constantly in the grip of death, the last word of biblical ethics is hope. Human knowledge and power, exercised in a spirit of stewardship and justice, can light up this dark earth. They are instrumentalities to keep hope alive. Ameliorative action that saves life, fosters health, and animates reconciliation and peace can presage redemption when it is stimulated by resurrection hope and resistance to evil. "Resurrection is verified," writes Stringfellow, "where resistance to the demonic thrives."

Knowledge is the concomitant of hope. The point of this theological excursion is that we must take knowledge with utmost seriousness. We cannot continue to believe, as some blithely suggest, that knowledge is amoral, value-free. The argument that knowledge is value-neutral, that it is only technological or political misuse of knowledge that is good or evil, is naive. The knowledge that we are now developing is technology. The time between idea and application, which used to involve years, has collapsed into a moment. Whether it is patenting life or nuclear fission, you have to "do it to know it." Knowledge is technique.

How does knowledge born in hope impinge on the cases we have cited? How does knowledge shape the ethical requirement? Since Jean LeJunes' isolation of the Trisomy 21 chromosomal anomaly, we have been given prebirth anticipation of a baby with Down syndrome. When diagnostic knowledge is joined to the technique of amniocentesis, our foreknowledge becomes part of the moral equation. Amniocentesis today becomes part of a broader spectrum of knowledge, which eventually will tell us much about a person before he or she is born. Knowledge yielded by our glimpse into the fetal window now includes, or soon will include, inborn errors, chromosome defects, neural-tube defects, sex, the propensity to cancer, heart diseases, schizophrenia, and a host of other problems. These possible traits are made known by gross observation, and the diagnosis of chromosomal and hematologic markers.

This prescience and predictive knowledge is a two-edged sword. When joined with ameliorative power, it can lead to genetic medicine, intrauterine therapy, or preparation for the unusual events that are to follow. Genetic medicine will one day correct inborn errors of metabolism, perhaps even the devastating biochemical disturbances caused by deranged or abnormal genetic substance. The dawn of intrauterine therapy already includes draining hydrocephalus, detoxifying fetal kidneys, and correcting urinary tract obstruction. It is now moving to the point of removing the fetus to do bench surgery, then replanting the fetus in the womb. This skill is moving rapidly to the point where we can begin to speak of the fetus as a patient.[3]

Conversely, this knowledge can lead to the decision to abort, to despair at ever again having a healthy baby, to genetic hypochondria, that generalized fear which immobilizes some not only from transmitting life, but from living itself. With Down syndrome, there is much we know, but much more that we do not know. In prenatal diagnosis, we discover only the extra chromosome. The penetrance, severity of retardation, and presence of physical anomalies remain unknown. The prospective accomplishment, or ability of that life, as well as the potential burden, pain, suffering, and cost is unknown. The future of persons born with Down syndrome is different in Sweden, where they are productive citizens, working in the bicycle factories, than in America, where they often are institutionalized. Cross-cultural variations were expressed again recently when a majority of British physicians polled argued that infants with Down syndrome should be allowed to die if their parents could not care for them.[4] Biblical ethics, with its dyadic structure of natural-law foundation and eschatological drive that we have noted in our foundational analysis, brings to our decision both requirement and uncertainty, both confidence and risk. In most medical decisions, there is much more that is unknown than is known. Dr. and Mrs. Mueller, though well-trained and knowledgeable medical clinicians, were caught by surprise when the twins were born. Much about our life is completely out of our control. The command to live in trust and obedience is the command to live into the unknown in justice and mercy.

Not only do we often know too little, we often think we know too much. Moral gnosticism is the dangerous inversion of agnosticism. In the abortion case before us, we are confronted with the tendency of the human mind and spirit to absolutize good and evil. Assuming erroneously that one's mind can totally embrace the truth (as if anyone ever doubted that), or that "abortion is always murder" (if so, nature is killing us all the time), or in the mother's words, that "if God wants the pregnancy terminated, he'll cause the miscarriage" (here we have the Newtonian fallacy, which identifies God with natural process), all these simplifications are attempts of the human mind to unscrew the inscrutable, to freeze the dynamic, to reduce life to still-life, in Goethe's words, to demand that the moment stand still.

Knowledge, in summary, is a guide, however insufficient, into the truth and therefore into the way. Knowledge instructs ethical choice but never collapses the good into a calculation. Knowledge is an instrument of the human spirit animated in hope, activated in the crises of decision. While omniscience would provide moral certainty, science—even when amplified with our newfound prescience—gives only a glimpse and a hunch.

Freedom

Freedom is one of the great themes of humanistic and religious hope. It is the purpose and hoped-for result of education and spiritual growth. But freedom in and of itself is vacuous. It must be anchored in responsibility. Otherwise, freedom degenerates into the doctrine of autonomy, with its treacherous anthropology that sees persons as isolated, independent monads. Moral freedom is freedom in community, freedom in mutual service. In the Judeo-Christian tradition, we live and have our being through and for one another. Moral freedom is dependence and interdependence, rather than independence. The final misconstrual of Enlightenment ethics that we now witness is a "do your own thing" ethics. In actuality, our lives are not autonomous and isolated. We live in covenants of life, public collectivities, societal contracts. Martin Luther correctly translated the Hebrew Bible in Genesis—God creates *"Menschen"*—humanity.

In addition to the communal idea, the doctrine of liberty, springing from the work of John Stuart Mill, has accented the idea that one should be free to decide on one's own, without the tyranny or coercion of another's will. This doctrine has affinity with the theological doctrine of conscience, especially as described by Luther and the Reformers. The bearing that the doctrine of freedom has on our topic of life and health is captured in the following questions: Are we free to make life and take life? If we are free in this sense, what are the designs and constraints which shape this exercise?

The great minds of the ages have conceived of freedom as the ability to know the good and to will it. Plato and Aristotle, Paul and Augustine speak of freedom as acting in accord with one's reason and moral will, without external compulsion. Moral freedom, if you will, is bondage to the truth. Only such servitude protects us from subservience. Kant saw three great questions intertwining—*what can I know, what must I do, what can I hope?* But moral freedom has never been left undefined. We are not free to harm and kill. With the exception of libertarians such as Robert Nozick and Ayn Rand, the great thinkers have always construed freedom in terms of mutual obligation.

The Semitic philosophers, whose wisdom we explored in chapter 2, say that the foundation of both Greek and Christian thought on the nature of human freedom is the doctrine of the one and the many. Each person is unique because the multiplicity is the whole. The signature of my life is indispensable because without it, the whole organism of humankind lacks a strategic part. Here we have the foundation of the idea of each person as an unrepeatable and irreplaceable entity. How then do we make life and take life? We are to create life as if we are receiving it as a gift. We are to safeguard it as if it were not our own. When the time comes to deliver up our life, we are to relinquish it as if to the One who gave it to us in the first place. This would seem to summarize the biblical doctrine of the self as responsive and responsible being.

Rabbi Jakobovits summarizes the notion in *The Encyclopedia of Bioethics:*

Biblical law regards every human life as absolute and infinite value. By mathematical definition, infinity can no more be increased by multiplication than it can be reduced by division. Hence a physically or mentally handicapped life, in whatever state of disability, is worth no less than a full and healthy life. And by the same token, one person has exactly the same value as a million people.

Then quoting the Sanhedrin Talmud (4:5):

Therefore was but a single person originally created in the world. To teach that if any person has caused a single soul to perish, it is as if that person caused the whole world to perish, and if any person saves a single life, that person has saved the whole world.[5]

In addition to the limits of freedom which we voluntarily choose, we also face inevitable contingency. Much of this contingency remains, of course, in our power over birth and death. When you have fallopian-tube blockage, there is not a thing you can do to have your own biological baby, unless you can get doctors to put you on the list for in-vitro fertilization. Contraception is imperfect and risk-fraught. Coronary-vascular and neoplastic diseases hit most of us, and we have very little freedom to say no.

In spite of these constraints of morbidity and mortality, we are developing an awesome range of choice at the thresholds of birth and death. In-vitro and the other fertilization and gestation technologies, fetal diagnosis, fetal medicine, and the other perinatal technologies are impressive. They are not univocally good, but they are impressive. But the ironies are overwhelming. While we can make babies in these exotic ways, we cannot control the moral disaster of 30 to 60 percent illegitimate births in our major cities. Abortion is widespread, while parents wishing to adopt cannot find a baby.

What is the meaning of responsible use of freedom in the covenants of care in which we live? The Sunday *New York Times* (November 15, 1981) had a full page ad from the New York coalition of religious groups for freedom of choice. Freedom of choice, they argued, is as sacred as the freedom of religion. To me, these arguments seem as misdirected as those of the Catholic bishops. I think we can opt in public policy for either option, and be on solid ethical ground, but only if and when we accompany our policy with a commitment to provide for the well-being of those new lives we have freely brought into the world. The ambivalence of freedom that we find at the inception of life is found also in those situations where we call upon life-support technologies. The techniques of dialysis, plasmapheresis, surgery, antibiotic therapy, cardiovascular and psychiatric therapy verge on the miraculous. Yet here too there are ironies. We seem impotent to do anything against the great vectors of morbidity and mortality: smoking and the abuse of alcohol and drugs. We have laid hold of great healing power with the free exercise of our knowledge and technology. At the same time, we seem powerless to control the behavioral freedom we have achieved. Here again, as Niebuhr would say, we find empirical verification for the primary fact of human life—that is, the misuse of freedom (sin). That ambiguous freedom, so exquisitely debated by Paul and the Judaizers, Luther and Erasmus, and the behaviorists and volitionists of our day, is a freedom characterized by creative possibility and constraint.

What does this concept of freedom imply for the cases under consideration? In the Down syndrome case, we find ourselves with a new quality of freedom that is both liberating and tragic. Amniocentesis conveys this poignant new quality of freedom. A former student of mine, a practicing OB gynecologist, called me one day. He and his wife have one beloved daughter who has Down syndrome. They speak of her as "the joy of their life," "the blessing of God." Now the wife is pregnant again. Reluctantly, they have decided to have the tests, since she felt she could not care for two exceptional children. But after she observed the well-formed baby on the sonogram, she came to her husband and said she could not go through with the tap, the amniocentesis, and the possible abortion. As she watched the movements, that little body within her made its claim on her heart. They had the tests anyway, and gratefully received the birth of a healthy son.

This quality of reluctant freedom is evidenced in the families I have met who have children with Down syndrome. Most of these families (caring, stable, and affluent) say that this child has graced their lives, *but* if they could prevent another such birth, they would. Bernard Häring, the great Dutch Catholic theologian, argues in the same spirit, that we may not have the right to knowingly bring defective children into the world. If Häring is correct, then this new juncture of knowledge and freedom creates a new responsibility. To knowingly bring a child with serious defects into the world is a morally different act than passively and innocently accepting this life. While it is stretching a point to argue that going ahead with the birth of a known defective child entails willful harm, we definitely must come to terms with what Tristram Engelhardt and others are labeling "wrongful life" or "the injury of prolonged existence."

These novel jurisprudential concepts are not nearly as problematic as Bentley Glass's construal of this avoidance of harm into a positive right. Glass has spoken of the "right of a child to be born normal" or "the right of every child to be born with the assurance of genes entitling him or her to adequate health and intelligence."

While free and responsible intelligence requires that we voluntarily pursue this goal, I am deeply distrustful of public policy in this area. Societal efforts to discard the defective, to make legal awards in wrongful life cases, or to begin either positive or negative eugenic campaigns is highly dubious activity. Margery Shaw, the physician-lawyer, contends that genetic disease is communicable disease, transmitted even more predictably than infectious disease. It should therefore be quarantined as a public-health measure. The immediate question that arises when this argument is presented is that which asks, Who is genetically healthy? Is the person with genetically based hyperlipoproteinemia, the propensity to turn inhaled smoke into a carcinogenic substance, a danger to society?

The best definition of a genetically healthy individual would be the person who is at peace and lives in gentle reciprocity with the ecosphere. The most genetically unhealthy, and therefore dangerous to the ecosphere of life, are certainly not persons with Down syndrome or achondroplastic dwarfs. They are people like us—intelligent, aggressive, consuming Western people. We ravenously devour the resources of this earth and despoil its fragile envelope of life-support. Ours are the dangerous genes that should not be allowed to proliferate. When Shockley announces that his sperm is on deposit at a California sperm bank, available to young women who wish to inseminate themselves with Nobel prize seed, I think of George Bernard Shaw's words to a chic London socialite at a party one night. The lady suggested that a planned offspring between them would be ideal.

Just think, she said, "My body and your brains."

"Yes, my dear," replied the decrepit old man, "but what if it had my body and your brains?"

Turning to the Siamese twin case, it too focused on the politics of freedom. The attending physician, with the consent of the parents, initially felt free not to initiate life-sustaining activities: suction, hydration, feeding, rejuvenation of the weaker twin. Several persons—a guilt-stricken nurse, a bureaucratic department of Children and Family Services, an aggressive state's attorney—felt that they, in freedom, could not allow this to go on. Both parties appealed to ethics and the law to undergird their conviction. Principles invoked included the freedom to practice medicine without political interference, parental freedom, and the societal liberty to protect life.

In the abortion case, we again deal with freedom and coercion. The question of minor status and parental justification is essentially a question of freedom. What is required today is freedom from the law, so that we can morally differentiate abortion cases along a spectrum. It is absurd to say that abortion is always right or always wrong. We need to distinguish kinds of situations where the technique of abortion will be called into play. Then, in a nuanced way, we can assign value or disvalue to a given case, according to some balance of principles of beneficence, no-maleficence, justice, and freedom.

Across the years, I have argued for a nuanced view of abortion, rejecting "right to life" and "freedom of choice" ideologies. I propose a sample spectrum: Some cases where *abortion is obligatory* are incest, child rape, and known profound genetic defects (Tay-Sachs disease, Lesch-Nyhan syndrome, for example). *Abortion is permissible, but not obligatory* in coercive out-of-wedlock pregnancy, moderately severe genetic or congenital abnormalities discovered in the fetus (Siamese twins, spina bifida, Down syndrome, and the like). *Abortion is permissible but discouraged* in illegitimate pregnancies, mild and treatable genetic or congenital accidents (hare lip, cleft palate, and the like). *Abortion is discouraged* for reasons of family hardship, unwanted or unplanned pregnancies, or birth control. *Abortion is proscribed* for reasons of convenience, population control, and sex selection.

This proposal betrays the fact that I am not happy with either the "right to life" or "freedom of choice" doctrine. Both are absolutistic abandonments of the subtleties of freedom and responsibility. I take it that our society is now groping for some nuanced abortion policy that will more appropriately honor our cultural values of "sanctity of life," freedom, and justice. I hope we reject the morally simplistic reduction of this complex of issues into the "right to life," "life begins at conception" configuration, on the one hand, and the equally absurd "freedom of choice" doctrine on the other. For the tragic interim, we need some nuanced public policy such as I have suggested, until completely reliable birth-control pills and vaccines are available and used. We have considered the moral burden of knowledge and the moral use of freedom.

Power

I return to the ethical themes set out earlier in this book. Biblical ethics and the theology of hope are about power. The Bible is about the power of God, which drives and determines the shape of history and human destiny. It is about Jesus Christ, in whom powerlessness is transfigured into the ruling power of the cosmos (Colossians 1). Biblical ethics is apocalyptic and eschatologic. It involves resistance, creative action, and patient waiting. This balanced notion of responsibility is best captured in a prayer by Reinhold Niebuhr:

> Lord, grant me the serenity to accept the things I cannot change, the courage to change the things that can be changed, and the wisdom to know the difference.

Knowledge-grounded, freedom-activated human power is a wonderful and frightful thing. It has yielded the ability to purify a water supply, to vaccinate for polio, to soar into heaven on a spaceship. We are the inheritors of the Puritan hope, a vision of a new millennium, a thrilling new world, ushered in by discovery and imagination. Milton wrote:

> Nature would surrender to humankind as its appointed governor, and human rule would extend from command of the earth and seas to dominion over the stars.[6]

Yet a dark cloud hovers on the horizon. Speaking of the new genetics, Robert Sinsheimer said, "We don't know which we face: an ambush or an epic opportunity."

My colleague at the University of Illinois, Dr. Chakrabarty, is patenting new life-forms: oil-eating and oil-producing organisms. It may be that we will need the former to save us from the latter. A sense of hesitancy and trembling now grips the scientific community. Ethics is the only growth industry in biomedicine, and we in that field are not serving the human prospect well at all. We are too pessimistic and naive. We rehearse ad nauseam the time-worn categories of moral analysis: deontology, utility, rights and risks, language and feelings, while the issues surge along at much deeper levels.

Today, our power moves deeper (with nuclear power), we threaten the very future of life on this planet. Soon we may hear the call that Noah heard, to create the ark of life to survive the deluge, this time a scorching radiation holocaust. The ark may indeed be Bentley Glass's subterranean bank of germ plasma. This time, the whole ark need not be the smelly mess with two elephants, two rhinos, and so on, but with germ cells and embryos in test tubes.

We are rapidly acquiring the power to change human nature itself. Perhaps it will be germ-cell genetics that will create a human chimera or clone. Perhaps neurochemistry will fundamentally alter the structure and function of the brain/mind. Perhaps biochemical modification will reverse the mechanisms of aging. Perhaps disease and death will be vanquished, and the remaining agony will be infinite boredom. Perhaps a human-machine chimera or a complete cyborg will achieve immortality. Humanity, as a singular, historic, and temporal organic entity, may give way to some grand or grotesque *übermensch*, superhuman.

This apocalyptic future may await us unless we learn to fulfill the requirements of justice, mercy, peace, and hope, the imperatives of our ethical heritage. The biomedical sphere is a good place to start. The dramas of life and death, of birth and suffering, those moments when we all confront existence stripped of pretense, provide a context in which we can remain fallen and damned humans, or where vulnerability and grace finally can begin to display our humanity. Unless we learn the grace to love and live for one another, even though we die, an ominous future awaits us. If we succeed, the glorious promise of *shalom*, where knowledge of God begins to cover the earth as the waters cover the sea, will come to us. If not, if we continue on our present path, we shall become those last spirits of Jude's vision:

> These are blemishes on your love-feasts . . . . They are waterless clouds carried along by the winds; autumn trees without fruit, twice dead, uprooted; wild waves of the sea, casting up the foam of their own shame; wandering stars, for whom the deepest darkness has been reserved forever.
>
> (Jude 12*b*-13 NRSV)

This morning a child born with Down syndrome enters this strange and wonderful world; another is lost forever. This morning other conjoined twins, oxygenated and intubated, living though dying, play and eat and struggle along in their hospital bedroom. This morning another young girl in Oklahoma prepares to have a baby. Microcosms of life, these cases have captured our attention. They symbolize the moral struggles we all face individually and collectively.

We have explored with illustration three ethical principles that proceed from the spirit of good, justice, and hope, which our moral history has focused from hybrid cultural roots onto modern natality bioethics. We now move to a concluding section, in which we will return to the specific features of the biomedical quest for life and health, and relate specific moral values to those concrete projects.

Mortality Ethics

Pontiac, Michigan (Spring 1996)

"My intent," said Dr. Kevorkian, "was to relieve pain, not to cause death." As a Michigan court exonerated him of two assists in dying in 1993, they did not accept this illogical argument or the frightening claim that he was "implementing justice," but rather the court decided on the fundamental human right to decide measures to be employed or forgone as one is dying. Ironically and coincidentally, a federal appeals court in San Francisco struck down the State of Washington's ban on physician-assisted suicides, finding that it violated a person's constitutional "right to die." Employing fundamental rights of the Constitution, derived from the theistic value heritage we have surveyed, as amplified by the Enlightenment doctrine of humanistic rights, the court said that the State's responsibility did not extend "when patients are no longer able to pursue liberty or happiness and do not wish to pursue life." As we noted previously, modern secular ethics are a stream fed by deep theological currents and the streams of contemporary humanistic enlightenment.

Kevorkian's several assisted suicides, all the doctor-assisted deaths in the American Northwest, even the few thousand persons euthanized in Holland, are not a statistically significant number. The significance of this cultural development is that our society is struggling legally, yes, but more basically, ethically and spiritually, with a right and good way to achieve and receive death. Dr. Ahi Khalili's dying, assisted by Dr. Kevorkian, had a profound impact on Chicago, the Midwest, and the nation. A revered physician, expert in rehabilitative and palliative care, a compassionate doctor to those who suffered in myriad ways, Khalili himself was dying from a disease that even my conservative teacher, Paul Ramsey, found an acceptable ground for assistance—metastatic bone cancer.

After consulting the world's leading cancer and pain experts (his own specialty), he decided that bringing an end to the process of excruciating suffering was ethically legitimate and personally responsible. We might ask why such a physician, with access to drugs, did not quietly and discretely take his own life and not resort to implicating another, namely Dr. Kevorkian. From what we can reconstruct, Dr. Khalili also wanted to make an ethical statement and contribute to what he saw as a crucial public debate. The deeper issue raised by these cases is to evaluate the morality and spirituality of intended death.

In this chapter, I will morally evaluate the phenomenon of "intending death." I will first argue that the intention to die gains some moral legitimacy because of developments in the contemporary culture. Some departure from our tradition which prohibits the intention to die is therefore called for. Second, I will cite several dangers implicit in this departure from the tradition and argue for caution. Finally, I will suggest that these developments intensify the need for informed and competent pastoral care. In all mortality, decisions of the kind of comprehensive ethic we have sketched are now required.

I. LEGITIMACY OF THE INTENTION TO DIE

The moral heritage of our culture finds the intention of death unacceptable. It is alien to the tradition. It is the antithesis of the hope for, right to, and love of life. To take one's life, to wish one were dead, or to request death for one whom we represent is medically, legally, and spiritually speaking, sickness, crime, and sin. Medical doctors and psychiatrists are trained to identify a desire for death as abnormal; the result of disrupted body chemistry, drug influence, debilitating pain, temporary insanity, or the green apples you ate. They are licensed to thwart this intention with injections, psychotherapy, behavior modification, or straps, straitjackets and padded cells. As far as the law is concerned, although suicide no longer carries the punishment of decapitation, disinheritance, and burial outside the Friedhof, the place of peace, we are most reticent to give people the right or the liberty to die. Our confused jurisprudence that results in inconsistent law is reflected in the oscillation of case law in Michigan's ethical meandering on the case of Dr. Kevorkian, and in the public policy on assisted dying in California, Washington, and Oregon.

Theology inherits the Sinai tradition, much compromised especially by those who wear the badge of Sinai and Golgotha, "Thou shall not kill." Yet we can and do. The politician Lyndon LaRouche is right when he claims that society is already singling out some groups for increased mortality: the aged poor and poor unwed pregnant mothers; the economics of our health care and welfare programs. It appears that we indeed can hasten or delay death's call. But should we? Does our dominion extend over our own body? Do we have the right to life or death over others? The heart of this whole tradition is that death stings because we love life. We feel obligated to protect one another from inflicted and intended death. This impulse roots our social contract. To illustrate the shape of the tradition, recall Blackstone's *Commentary on the Law of England:*

> Self-murder, the pretended heroism but real cowardice of the Stoic philosophers who destroyed themselves to avoid those ills which they had not the fortitude to endure. The law of England wisely and religiously concurs that no man hath a power to destroy life but by commission from God, the author of it, and as their suicide is guilty of a double offense, one spiritual, in evading the prerogative of the Almighty and rushing into his immediate presence uncalled for, the other temporal against the King, who hath an interest in the preservation of all his subjects.[7]

One composite ethical tradition also conveys limitations and the awareness of finitude. Today there are reasons to modify this composite tradition—to differentiate qualities of the "intention to die," to open up options in medical practice, legal practice, and pastoral ministry to understand, allow, perhaps even encourage and help persons who wish to die. This should be done only with the gravest reservation and deepest reverence for personal life. There are times and circumstances when we must recognize exceptions to our inherited moral wisdom. What developments make this necessary? I mention four reasons: (1) life-prolonging techniques; (2) the economy of living; (3) iatric disease; and (4) common sense.

1. One such development is the panorama of life-prolonging techniques. These range from functional supports like mechanical respirators to sophisticated abilities to supply and control the element of vitality: electrolytes, metabolites, salts, fluids, nutrients, blood components. Sometimes medicine can slam the door on death for the time being with these techniques. Other times, he keeps his foot in the door and our ministrations only prolong dying. Some would argue today that with thousands of Karen Quinlans lying near and far, we have, for the first time in human history, made it possible for us to outlive ourselves.

2. The second argument must be used with utmost caution. It has to do with the economy of life. We live in families, in towns, in societies, on a globe with limited resources. Savings run out. Anyone of my age who has any confidence that Social Security, Medicare or Medicaid will still be there when we retire is a fool. And should society expend so much of its youth, its wealth, its energy in attending the sick, the disabled, the dying? Should college plans be dropped, family life destroyed, the lives of caretakers shortened, because of the sheer weight of attending a loved one? The desire to do everything possible is a questionable motive. Sometimes wanting the very most, the very best for our dying friends and relations is only satiating our own guilt for ignoring them while they were living. We very likely need to learn the first skill of life saving, which is self-preservation, and not feel guilty about it. We may need to hear a fresh command in Jesus' words, "Let the dead bury their dead."

3. A third circumstance that renders death-acceptance or death-election a different kind of question today is the changing face of disease. Much illness today is *iatric*, man-made. We have polluted all that we breathe, drink, and ingest. Our indulgent, indolent, and frantic lifestyles have triggered new plagues of vascular disease, cancer, and now epidemic depression and senile dementia. In some future day, we might find that all our illnesses and deaths are self-elected. In light of this, it might be argued that we have already chosen modes of self-destruction, and it would be absurd to now introduce at death's threshold heroic countermeasures—costly, caustic extensions and intensifications of the suffering we have deliberately chosen.

4. Fourth, there is the wisdom of simple *common sense*. Futurists have argued that in the future we will live for 150 years, immunized against all diseases, anesthetized from all pain, able to hibernate for decades or centuries if we desire. But rather than exulting in such prospects, we find them boring and sad. People don't want to be immortal, at least when the wish is actualized. There was a woman who received one wish from the gods; at first impulse she requested immortality, then spent the rest of eternity yearning that she might die. Seneca, in his tract on suicide, wrote, "The wise man lives as long as he should, not as long as he can." And G. B. Shaw, that saintly cynic of our generation, writes in the *Doctor's Dilemma:*

> Do not try to live forever, you will not succeed. Use your health even to the point of wearing it out. That is what it is for. Spend all you have before you die, and do not outlive yourself.[8]

II. PRECAUTIONS

There are certain inherent dangers in the tendency to qualify the tradition and welcome death. Let me cite several developments that signal the shift. There is a widespread tendency in our culture to naturalize death and discern the dying process in terms of predictable stages. Simple schemata are as dangerous for petite functionaries in health care as in education. They start believing in the stages. The Beatrix Cobb/Elisabeth Kübler-Ross sequence of pre- and post-death stages has been criticized for its Greek naturalism, which strips death and immortality of its rich senses of terror and mystery, meanings implicit in Hebrew-Christian hope. Studies show that today's physicians do not fear death as did their fathers. We might see this total development as a maturation of our views, a diminishing of our repressions, a step forward. Why do I suggest implicit danger in the cultural tendency to allow, even assist in death? Let me mention a cultural argument, an argument from the psychic-emotional nature of man, concluding with a theological point.

Cultural Tendencies   Thomas Hardy paints the plight of modern "unnoticed" man in his 1890 novel, *Jude the Obscure.* Jude and Susan have just discovered the lifeless bodies of the two children and son, Jude, hanging in the chamber room of the inn where they are staying. The boy has left a note saying, "we are too many." Susan blames herself because she spoke with young Jude of the impending burden with a new child on the way.

"No," said Jude. "It was in his nature to do it. The doctor says there are such boys springing up amongst us—boys of a sort unknown in the last generation—the outcome of new views of life. They seem to see all its terrors before they are old enough to have staying power and resist them. He says it is the beginning of the coming universal wish not to live." [9]

Important sociological studies today are showing that the technological cultures of the West, shaped by the secularistic worldviews derivative of Protestant religious traditions, are dramatically shifting the balance of "intended death" away from homicide to suicide. Death claims us in three ways: accidents, natural death from illness, and intended death—homicide and suicide. Of the total mortality, intended death is increasing in percentage along with accidents, which have certain affinities to both suicide and homicide. Death from natural causes alone is diminishing proportionally.

One might interpret this as a profound cultural phenomenon, related to certain biological adaptations to environments that have limited carrying capacities. In any animal population, crowding results in diminished fertility and heightened violence, including self-destruction.

The import of this point for our discussion is only to show a tendency in our culture to rationalize the wish to die, or the intention to bring death to others, as something natural, even noble. Awareness of this phenomenon should heighten our critical scrutiny of right-to-die proposals in the spheres of personal life choice and public policy.

Human Emotions   We must also examine the emotional structure of human life. Here also we find reason for caution as we seek to morally affirm the "intention of death." Wanting to die can often, though not always, proceed from the collapse of hope. Hope is born in self-esteem, seeing one's life as meaningful, having a sense that one's existence has purpose. Jürgen Moltmann has shared, in a recent conversation, his experience of fifteen-year-old recruits to Hitler's army during the waning days of the Third Reich. They were willing to die, courageous, blind to danger, because they hated themselves. Those not afraid to die often have "love failure"—the joy and sustenance of loving and being loved has collapsed. Death comes quite smoothly, quite naturally to those who have fallen out of love.

Understanding human emotions, wherein love and fear of death are joined, as are loss and willingness to die, helps us to be personally more sensitive and tough. Sometimes the statement, "I wish mother could be spared this pain and suffering" means, "I'm weary and want to go home." Sometimes the cry, "I'm sick to death and am going to end it all" means "Help!" There are times when the intention to die, the willingness to die, even the merciful desire to end one's misery, or that of another, flows from mature decision, love of life and self—not hatred. Here we should stand near in support. But often the motives are mixed and confused. Here we need the staying power to struggle through the conflict with another. Sometimes the motives are sheer selfishness, expediency, institutional efficiency, or creature comfort. The worse thing we can do is applaud this "sickness unto death." Here we should resist and rush in with aid, knowing the enduring bitterness and pain of conscience that follow such decisions to let go.

A Theological Caution   Sweet death comes hard. Theology has always known this. Paraphrasing Dietrich Bonhoeffer from his sojourn in Spain, it is only when one loves this life and this earth so much that without them everything would be lost and gone—only when one cherishes this life can one believe in the resurrection. Pagan notions of immortality still tease our culture. How many times have we been assaulted by our parishioners when we challenge the notion of the immortal soul! Death for the Christian is total, final, body and spirit. The soul does not float out to rejoin the great soul. We affirm the resurrection of the body.

Oscar Cullmann has sketched their difference by contrasting the deaths of Socrates and Jesus. Plato's account of the death of Socrates in the *Phaedo* sublimely expresses the Greek notion of the immortality of the soul. The essence of the belief is that the mortal physical body must be shed as an outer garment, that the essential soul can be liberated to its eternal home. Death is good and natural, because it releases the soul from its prison in the body. The body can be destroyed; the soul is eternal. Those who describe the natural stages of death, and speak of death as part of life, are invoking once again this Greek sense of immortality.

Jesus, by contrast, approaches his death with trembling and distress (see Mark 14:33, 15:34; Luke 12:50). Jesus is afraid of impending death, sharing as he does man's natural fear. In the Semitic perception, death is dreadful and terrifying. Jesus cries to be released from "this cup" (Mark 14:36). Death is an enemy of man, an enemy of God. It is the last enemy to be destroyed (1 Corinthians 15:26). It is not the natural order of things. Man dies because of his sin; Jesus dies atoning for man's sin. Only in Jesus as Christ is death stripped of its terror. Now, although man must taste death, it has no sting. The shadowy belief in resurrection in Hebrew faith now becomes a full-flown hope in the resurrection into life.

III. PASTORAL MANDATE

The present revisions of our "winnowed wisdom," tempered by the cautions proposed for cultural, personal, and theological reasons, will work only if we reaffirm the ancient impetus to care for the dying with pastoral tenderness. Cicero saw life as a sober, yet joyous task, "dying men caring for dying men." The medieval and Renaissance world studied the art of dying. Today, with our tendencies to regularize, institutionalize, codify death, to make it a noun, together with the inclination to abandon, hide, and camouflage those who are dying, we might profitably examine with a pastoral eye our "death policies and practices."

We must agree with Ivan Illich when he claims that a society's understanding of death also controls its understanding of health. An indicative characteristic of our culture is the fact that in cocktail-party chatter, sex and death are no longer repressed subjects— indeed, they are the hors d'oeuvres, the subject of unending banter. Religion is the repressed, forbidden topic. Even the presidential candidates who, by disposition, would love to talk about their faith, are warned by their advisors to contain it—talk about morality, integrity, of course, but not religion. The unreality of our culture is seen when, in death, we can speak only of life: "Oh, you'll be all right"; "How are you?"; "Come on now—chin up." And in life, we can speak only of death. Nietzsche is a helpful corrective at this point:

> The Thought of Death.—It gives me melancholy happiness to live in the midst of this confusion of streets, of necessities, of voices; how much more enjoyment, impatience, and desire, how much thirsty life and drunkenness of life comes to light here every moment! And yet it will soon be so still for all these shouting, lively, life-loving people! How everyone's shadow, his gloomy traveling companion stands behind him! It is always as in the last moment before the departure of an emigrant-ship; people have more than ever to say to one another, the hour presses, the ocean with its lonely silence waits impatiently behind all the noise—so greedy, so certain of its prey! And all, all, suppose that the past has been nothing, or a small matter, that the near future is everything: hence this haste, this crying, this self-deafening and self-overreaching! Everyone wants to be foremost in this future—and yet death and the stillness of death are the only things certain and common to all in this future! How strange that this sole thing that is certain and common to all exercises almost no influence on men, and that they are the furthest from regarding themselves as the brotherhood

of death! It makes me happy to see that men do not want to think at all of the idea of death! I would fain do something to make the idea of life even a hundred times more worthy of their attention.[10]

Pastoral care, leading one another to water, restoring souls in conviviality, making to lie down in green pastures, leading beside still waters, bridging over troubled waters, preparing tables, anointing with oil—these arts ancient and blessed—must be relearned. Above all, we must gently undershepherd one another to that Great Shepherd of the sheep.

> *Schafe können sicher weiden*
> *wo ein guter Hirte wacht.*
> ("Sheep may safely graze,"
> J. S. Bach, Cantata #9.)

– STUDY GUIDE –

I ndividuals and groups may use the following lead questions to
quide them through this study. Discussion and debate on each
question should fill a discussion hour for each chapter:

- How is the grand biomedical quest a worthy (unworthy) ambition?
- What does the Greek concept of nature contribute to our
  worldview?
- Is apocalyptic consciousness a good and healthy part of our ethical apparatus? What does it signal to us about norms and values?
- What unique perspectives on reality (time and space) are
  afforded by Christianity?
- Relate the sublime ethical distillation of the Decaloque to the
  human quest for well-being. Consider both imperatives and
  prohibitives of the biblical "Way of Life."
- Now does "natural law" contribute and detract from the human
  ethics of well-being?
- If the apocalyptic assertion is correct and we humans are suspended between time and eternity, nature and transcendence,
  what is the nature of our moral responsibility?
- In the kingdom of God that Jesus makes our hope, what shall
  we live and work for in the realm of well-being?
- What hopes shall we pursue (and reject) in the realm of birth
  ethics?
- What hope shall we pursue (and reject) in the realm of death
  ethics?

— CONCLUSION —

H his book is the result of three decades of involvement in the scientific and technological institutions that so pro-founumankind came silently into the world," writes Teil-hard. Humanity threatens to go out with a bang, perhaps a whim-per. This book has suggested that if we pause for a moment, we will understand where we came from, what has made us who we are, and why we remain *Homo Viator*, humans on the Quest. The question now becomes one of laying hold of the "why" that underlies our nature and history, and then activating that wisdom within our technical enterprise. We will have no certainty of the wisdom of our course. We will be buffeted by "people of sense" because of the elusiveness of our visions and dreams. We will pur-sue and endure, hope driving our quest. We may prevail. We may fail. Yet when all is said and done, we will know when the human story is consummated that "the world was better for this."

– POSTSCRIPT –

We will soon awake to a new day, January 1, 2000. It will be just another day like any other. A new year, decade, century, millennium. Stuck as we are in *chronos*—measured time bits and sound bites—will go on. Slight reflection will reveal the momentous. *Kairos* hovers in the shadows. The reader will have come to expect such gibberish from a scholar who gives intellectual credence and ethical credit not only to the data of nature and history, but to the data of apocalyptic and the eschato-logic. Yet, it is just the turn into another millennium in one of the calendars that cross off days. Remember that for the Jewish, Chinese, and Islamic calendar, 2000 C.E. is just another odd year. But deeper reflection tells another story. Human history has entered a cataclysmic phase, and the momentum and dynamic can be traced along the epochs we have identified with Hebraic, Greek, apocalyptic and Christic moral consciousness. Something novel, abrupt, and profoundly salient has come into the world's saga and is found along the pathways we call Semitic, classic, Christian, Renaissance, and modern history.

This book has argued that this composite and integral world-view has fashioned a way with the world—a human technological endeavor. This quest has been, and will continue to be punctuated by ethical decisions of enormous import. I have contended that moral guidance sufficient to the task is imbedded in the same history of consciousness and consciousness that gave rise to the technology. We have traced the lineaments of that moral consciousness and the derivative technological venture. Although we have surveyed the broad contours of that technology, we have focused on the quest for life and health.

As we close out one millennium and open another (in the

Christic now called common era) an overt paradise with ominous clouds seems to unfold before us. An adequate food supply for the global family now seems possible, yet the northwest salmon are threatened, and water supplies in the Midwest are contaminated from toxic farm run-off. In Rwanda in Africa, Somalia in the Mediterranean, and even Bosnia in Europe, people have only recently starved along the streets. Human cloning now seems frighteningly immanent in a Scottish sheep called "Dolly." Childhood cancers have been impressively fathomed and fought, yet oncogenetic devastation persists, even intensifies. Smallpox, leprosy, and many infections have been cornered, then eradicated, yet HIV and other sexually transmitted diseases abound, Eboli and other frightening mutant bacteria and fungi arise into human flesh, and persistent potentially remedial plagues—river blindness, schistosomiasis, chronic diarrhea—devastate the world's poor, especially children. Rienhold Niebuhr's prognosis of progress seems borne out: the world is simultaneously becoming better and better, and worse and worse.

The saga of impressive history is therefore a call that we have become responsible for the future of life and the world. What is to become of the world has increasingly become our charge. That is the dramatic new fact. Something is wrong. Something could be better. We can do something about it. We can exert our power over conception, birth, and death. This, in part, is novel. We can steer the development of the world along paths of equity, freedom, and distributive justice, or along the prevalent paths of greed and concentration of wealth and privilege. This is categorically a new human competency. Humanity has, in the words of martyr Dietrich Bonhoeffer, "come of age."

– Notes –

Introduction

1 Herman Kahn and Anthony Wiener, *The Year 2000: A Framework for Speculation on the Next Thirty-three Years* (New York: Macmillian, 1967).

2 René Dubos and Barbara Ward, *Only One Earth* (New York: Norton, 1972).

3 Theodore Roszak, *Where the Wasteland Ends* (New York: Doubleday, 1972). See also his earlier work, *The Making of a Counter-Culture* (New York: Doubleday, 1969).

4 Charles Reich, *The Greening of America* (New York: Random House, 1970). See also the collection of commentary, Philip Nobile, ed., *The Con III Controversy: The Critics Look at the Greening of America* (New York: Pocket Books, 1971).

5 Jay Forrester, *World Dynamics* (Cambridge, Mass.: Wright-Allen Press, 1971). See also Donella H. Meadows, Dennis L. Meadows, Jørgen Randers, William W. Behrens III, *The Limits to Growth* (London: Earth Island Press, 1972).

6 Herbert Marcuse, *One-Dimensional Man* (Boston: Beacon Press, 1964); Derek J. De Solla Price, *Little Science, Big Science* (New York: Columbia University Press, 1963).

7 Kenneth Vaux, ed., *To Create a Different Future* (New York: Friendship Press, 1972).

8 P. J. Thung, "Man and Science: The Crisis in Confidence," *Anticipation* No. 1 (April 1970). Published by the Department of Church and Society, The World Council of Churches, p. 3.

9 Wolf-Dieter Marsch, "Technology and the Future in a Theological Perspective," *Anticipation* No. 5 (Dec. 1970), p. 12.

10 The titles that summarize the best theological and technological work in this field: Alvin Toffler, *The Futurists* (New York: Random House, 1972); Ewert H. Cousins, ed., *Hope and the Future of Man* (Philadelphia: Fortress Press, 1972).

11 Emil Brunner, *Christianity and Civilization*, Vol. II (London: Nisbet & Co. 1949), p. 4.

12 Martin Marty, *The Search for a Usable Future* (New York: Harper & Row, 1969), pp. 26-27.

13 Mircea Eliade, *The Quest: History and Meaning in Religion* (Chicago: University of Chicago Press, 1969), pp. 87, 90.
14 Reinhold Niebuhr, *Moral Man in Immoral Society* (New York: Scribners, 1932), p. 93.

Chapter 1. The Hope for Well-Being and the Goals of Medicine

1 Alfred North Whitehead, *Science and the Modern World* (Cambridge University Press, 1953), p. 15.
2 Michael DeBakey, "The Medical Prognosis: Favorable, Treatable, Curable," *Saturday Review World* (August 24, 1974), p. 46.
3 *U.S. News and World Report* (March 3, 1975), p. 46.
4 Noah Webster, "Letters on Yellow Fever Addressed to Dr. William Currie," *Supplements to the Bulletin of the History of Medicine*, ed. Henry E. Sigerist (Baltimore: Johns Hopkins Press, 1947), p. 34.
5 Jürgen Moltmann, *Theology of Hope* (New York: Harper & Row, 1964), p. 25.
6 Bentley Glass, "The Ethical Basis of Science," *Science* (150) 1965, p. 1258.
7 "An Essay on Religion, Death, and Evolutionary Adaptation," *Zygon* (December 1966), p. 331.
8 *U.S. News and World Report* (March 3, 1975), p. 43.
9 "Hope and the Biomedical Future of Man," *Hope and the Future of Man*, ed. Ewert H. Cousins (Philadelphia: Fortress Press, 1972), p. 104.

Chapter 2. Formative Influences on Our Technological and Ethical Consciousness

1 Ernst Bloch, *Atheism in Christianity* (New York: Herder & Herder, 1972), p. 9.
2 Rudolf Bultmann, *History and Eschatology: The Presence of Eternity* (New York: Harper, 1957), p. 6.
3 Miller Burrows, "Ancient Israel," *The Idea of History in the Ancient Near East* (New Haven: Yale University Press, 1955), p. 107.
4 René Dubos, *Mirage of Health* (New York: Doubleday, 1959).
5 William Foxwell Albright, *New Horizons in Biblical Research* (London: Oxford University Press, 1966), p. 31.
6 Albert Speer, *Inside the Third Reich* (New York: Macmillan, 1970), pp. 112-13.
7 Buckminster Fuller, *Utopia or Oblivion* (New York: Bantam Books, 1969), pp. 290-91. Italics my additions.
8 Schubert Ogden, "The Temporality of God," *The Reality of God and Other Essays* (London: SCM Press, 1967), pp. 144ff.

9 Wolfhart Pannenberg, *Theology and the Kingdom of God* (Philadelphia: Westminster Press, 1969), p. 62

10 Paul Tillich, *A History of Christian Thought* (New York: Harper & Row, 1968), p. 11.

11 In my book *Subduing the Cosmos: Cybernetics and Man's Future* (Richmond, Va.: John Knox Press, 1970), emphasis was placed on secularization as the consciousness perquisite to the rise of science and technology. Equally important is the notion that the natural process is moral in character and that secularization does not exclude a sacralization of nature.

12 Albright, *New Horizons in Biblical Research*, p. 32.

13 Mircea Eliade, *The Quest: History and Meaning in Religion* (Chicago: University of Chicago Press, 1969), p. 3.

14 Mircea Eliade, *The Myth of the Eternal Return* (New York: Bollingen Foundation, 1954), p. 104.

15 Emil Brunner, *Christianity and Civilization, Vol. I* (London: Nisbet & Co., 1948), p. 50.

16 Arend Van Leeuwen, *Christianity in World History* (New York: Scribners, 1964); Carl F. von Weizsäcker, *The History of Nature* (Chicago: University of Chicago Press, 1949); Alfred North Whitehead, *Science and the Modern World* (Cambridge: University Press, 1953).

17 Whitehead, p. 15.

18 Weizsäcker has made this point in several conferences during the summer of 1972. His recent thought on the subject can be found in the essays of *Die Einheit der Natur* (München: Carl Hanser Verlag, 1971), pp. 441ff.

19 Edith Hamilton, the *Greek Way* (New York: Harper, 1930).

20 John McHale, *The Future of the Future* (New York: George Braziller, 1969), p. 26.

21 Francois Guerand, "Greek Mythology," *The New Larousse Encyclopedia of Mythology* (London: Paul Hamlyn, 1969), p. 93.

22 Whitehead, p. 12. For a discussion of the time concept in Greek Drama, see the study of Jacqueline de Romily, *Time in Greek Tragedy* (Ithaca: Cornell University Press, 1968).

23 Fred Polak, *Prognostics* (Amsterdam: Elsevier, 1971), pp. 61ff.

24 R. G. Collingwood, *The Idea of Nature* (Oxford: Clarendon Press, 1945), p. 3.

25 Plato, *The Republic: Bk. VII*, trans. A. D. Lindsey (London: Everyman's Library, 1935).

26 Weizsäcker, pp. 441ff.

27 Albert Einstein, "Science and Religion" (address at Princeton Theological Seminary, May 19, 1939) published in *Ideas and Opinions* (New York: Crown Publishers, 1954), pp. 41ff.

28 For an extended discussion of the current debate on the sources of Plato's *Timaeus*, see Theo Gerard Sinniga, *Matter and Infinity in the*

Presocratic Schools and Plato (Essen: Van Gorcum, 1968), p. 172. The Empedoclean background can be surveyed in the study by Joann Christoph Lirth, *Die Struktur des Weizäcker in Empedokleischen System "Uber die Natur"* (Meisenheim am Glan: Verlag Anton Hain, 1970).

29 W. D. Ross, ed., *Aristotle's Metaphysics* (Oxford: Clarendon Press, 1970), p. cxxxi.

30 Ibid., p. cl.

31 Ibid., p. cli. This concept is fully developed in *De Anima*.

32 See, for example, Whitehead, p. 219.

33 Alfred North Whitehead, *Process and Reality* (New York: Macmillan, 1969), p. 403.

34 Ibid., p. 215.

35 Tillich, p. 97.

36 Werner Heisenberg, *Der teil und Das Ganze* (Munchen: R. Piper, 1968).

37 Tillich, p. 107.

38 Ernst Benz, *Evolution and the Christian Hope* (Garden City, New York: Doubleday & Co., 1966), p. 9.

39 Ibid., p. 10.

40 Ibid., p. 11.

41 This interpretation of the French Revolution and subsequent Western History is presented in Michael Polanyi, "Beyond Nihilism," Marjorie Grene, ed., *Knowing and Being: Essays by Michael Polanyi* (London: Routledge & Kegan Paul, 1969), p. 3ff.

42 Benz, p. 12.

43 A. M. Klaus Müller, Wolfhart Pannenberg, *Erwägungen zu einer Theologie der Natur* (Munchen: Gutersloher Verlagshaus, 1970).

44 Martin Heidegger, in a personal letter to Klaus Mayer-Abich. Written in 1969, the text was supplied by the letter's recipient.

45 H. H. Rowley, *The Relevance of Apocalyptic* (London: Lutterworth Press, 1963), p. 171.

46 Ernst Käsemann, for example, has suggested the thesis that "apocalyptic is the mother of Christian theology." See Robert W. Funk, ed., *Apocalypticism* (New York: Herder & Herder, 1969).

47 Ernst Benz, *Evolution and Christian Hope* (Garden City: Doubleday, 1966). See in particular chapter 8, "The Christian Expectation of the End of Time and the Idea of Technical Progress."

48 Of all the literature on this theme, I would select Norman Perrin's *The Kingdom of God in the Teaching of Jesus* (London: SCM Press, 1966) and Joachim Jeremias, *The Parables of Jesus* (New York: Scribners, 1963). Bultmann stresses the radical existential character of the Kingdom. See, for example, Rudolf Bultmann, *History and Eschatology: The Presence of Eternity* (New York: Harper Torch Books, 1957). For an intriguing modern treatment of the historical-natural interpretation of Kingdom developed in apology for an ecological theology, see

H. Paul Santmire, *Brother Earth* (New York: Nelson Co., 1971), pp. 103ff.

49 John Dominic Crossan, *The Historical Jesus* (San Francisco: Harper, 1991). Philip Yancey, *The Jesus I Never Knew* (Grand Rapids: Zondervan, 1995).

50 Gustav Dalman, *Die Worte Jesu* (Leipzig: Schurr Verlag, 1930), p. 34.

51 Joseph Sittler, *Called to Unity* (Philadelphia: Muhlenberg Press, 1962).

52 For elaborations of this element, see N. A. Dahl, "The Parables of Growth" *Studia Theologica* (1957), pp. 132-66, and Dan Otto Via, *Die Gleichnisse Jesu* (München: Kaiser Verlag, 1970). See particularly the discussions of "cosmological parables." Also relevant are the Luke studies of Hans Conzelmann, *Die Mitte der Zeit* (Tübingen: Mohr, 1964).

53 Ernst Bloch, *Man on His Own* (New York: Herder & Herder, 1970), p. vi.

54 Rudolf Bultmann, *History and Eschatology: The Presence of Eternity* (New York: Harper Torchbooks, 1957), p. 47.

55 Wolfhart Pannenberg, *Theology and the Kingdom of God* (Philadelphia: Westminster Press, 1969), p. 111.

56 Eugene Rosenstock-Huessy, *Out of Revolution* (New York: Four Wells, 1964), p. 120.

57 Paul Tillich, *A History of Christian Thought* (New York: Harper & Row, 1968), p. 36.

58 Oscar Cullmann, *Christ and Time* (Philadelphia: Westminster Press, 1960), p. 41.

59 Johannes B. Metz, *Theology of the World* (New York: Herder & Herder, 1971), p. 49.

60 Paul Tillich, *A History of Christian Thought* (New York: Harper & Row, 1968), pp. 40, 41.

61 Ibid., pp. 63ff.

62 See, for example, Henry Adams, *From Mont St. Michel to Chartres* (New York: Doubleday, 1959) and Etienne Gilson, *Reason and Revelation in the Middle Ages* (New York: Charles Scribner's Sons, 1938).

63 Benz, *Evolution and Christian Hope*, p. 39.

64 For a discussion of the medieval beginnings of modern scientific and technological mentality, see Gunter Howe, *Gott und die Technik* (Hamburg: Furche Verlag, 1971), pp. 49ff.

65 Benz, *Evolution and Christian Hope*, p. 128.

66 A. N. Whitehead, *Science and the Modern World* (Cambridge: The University Press, 1953), p. 15.

67 Charles Rufus Morey, *Medieval Art* (New York: Norton, 1942), p. 277.

68 Jean Calvin, *Institutes of the Christian Religion, Bk. III* (Philadelphia: Westminster Press, 1960), p. 718.

69 James P. Martin, *The Last Judgment in Protestant Theology from Orthodoxy to Ritschl* (Grand Rapids: Eerdmans, 1963), p. 11.

70 Ibid, p. 27.
71 Tillich, *History of Christian Thought*, pp. 23, 24.
72 Karl Löwith, *Meaning in History* (Chicago: University of Chicago Press, 1949), p. 244.
73 Fred L. Polak, *Prognostics* (Amsterdam: Elsevier, 1971), p. 87.
74 Ralph Waldo Emerson, quoted in Leo Marx, *The Machine in the Garden: Technology and the Pastoral Ideal in America* (New York: Oxford University Press, 1964), pp. 192ff.
75 See for example, H. R. Niebuhr's study, *The Kingdom of God in America* (New York: Harper & Row, 1937).
76 For documentation, see Gösta Lundström, *The Kingdom of God in the Teaching of Jesus* (London: Oliver & Boyd, 1963).
77 Panenberg, *Theology and the Kingdom of God*, p. 114
78 Karl Barth, *The Epistle to the Romans* (Oxford: University Press, trans. E. C. Hoskyns, 1933), p. 314.
79 Ibid., p. 484.
80 "Christ—the Hope of the World" in *The Christian Hope and the Task of the Church: The Report of the Assembly Prepared by the Advisory Commission on the Main Theme, 1954* (New York: Harper & Bros., 1954), p. 1.
81 Ibid., p. 1.
82 Ibid., p. 2.
83 Ibid., p. 3.
84 Ibid., p. 3.
85 Ibid., p. 3.
86 Ibid., p. 6.
87 Ibid., p. 6.
88 Ibid., p. 6.
89 Ibid., p. 9.
90 Ibid., p. 13.
91 Ibid., p. 42.
92 Ibid., p. 47.
93 Michael Polanyi, "Beyond Nihilism," in Marjorie Grene, ed., *Knowing and Being* (London: Routledge & Kegan Paul, 1969), pp. 3ff.
94 Eugene Rosenstock-Huessy, *Out of Revolution*, pp. 365-66.
95 Carl Friedrich von Weizsäcker, *Die Einheit der Natur* (München: Carl Hauser Verlag, 1971), pp. 365ff.
96 See, at this point, Paul Tillich's discussion of the consequences of technical reason, leading to objectification and manipulation of the reality that is thus discerned in *Systematic Theology, Vol. V. III* (Chicago: University of Chicago Press, 1963), pp. 57ff.
97 Kenneth Keniston, *The Uncommitted: Alienated Youth in American Society* (New York: Harcourt Brace, 1960), pp. 93, 190.
98 Polak, *Prognostics*, p. 55, my italics.

Chapter 3. Derivative Ethical Axioms

1 Michael Polanyi, "Beyond Nihilism" in Marjorie Grene, ed. *Knowing and Being, Essays by Michael Polanyi* (London: Routledge & Kegan Paul, 1969), p. ix.

2 Carl Friedrich von Weizsäcker, *Zum Weltbild der Physik* (Stuttgart: S. Hirzel Verlag, 1954), pp. 264ff.

3 John McHale, *The Future of the Future* (New York: George Braziller, 1969), p. 9.

4 René Dubos, *Man Adapting* (New Haven: Yale University, 1965), p. 7.

5 John Cohen, "Subjective Time" from J. T. Fraser, ed., *The Voices of Time* (New York: George Braziller, 1967), p. 262.

6 Wolf-Dieter Marsch, "Technology and the Future in a Theological Perspective," *Anticipation* (Geneva: World Council of Churches, No. 5, Dec. 1970), p. 12.

7 See Lynn White, *Medieval Technology and Social Change* (New York: Oxford University Press, 1962).

8 Robert W. Prehoda, *Designing the Future: the Role of Technological Forecasting* (Philadelphia: Chilton Book Co., 1967), p. 7.

9 Wolfhart Pannenberg, "Future and Unity," Ewert H. Cousins, ed., *Hope and the Future of Man* (Philadelphia: Fortress Press, 1972), p. 74.

10 Martin P. Golding, "What Is Our Obligation to Future Generations?" *Working Paper of the Institute of Society, Ethics, and the Life Sciences* (New York: Hastings-on-Hudson, 1971), p. 7.

11 Jørgen Randers, "Global Limitations and Human Responsibility" in Kenneth Vaux, ed., *To Create a Different Future* (New York: Friendship Press, 1972), p. 38.

12 Jürgen Moltmann, *Hope and Planning* (New York: Harper & Row, 1971), p. 197.

13 Donella H. Meadows, Dennis L. Meadows, Jørgen Randers, William W. Behrens III, *The Limits to Growth* (London: Earth Island Publications, 1972), p. 24.

14 Ibid., p. 127.

15 Theodosius Dobzhansky, "Human Values in an Evolving World" in Cameron Hall, ed., *Human Values and Advancing Technology* (New York: Friendship Press, 1969), p. 64.

16 Robert Theobald, "Compassion or Destruction: Our Immediate Choice," in Hall, *Human Values and Advancing Technology*, pp. 32ff.

17 Geoffrey Vickers, *Value Systems and Social Process* (New York: Penquin Books, 1970), p. 41.

18 Lynn White, "Snake Nests and Icons," in *Anticipation: Christian Social Thought in Future Perspective*, No. 10 (Geneva: World Council of Churches, Feb. 1972), p. 31.

19 Charles West, "Theology and Technological Change," *Anticipation:*

Christian Social Thought in Future Perspective, No. 5 (Geneva: World Council of Churches, Dec. 1970) p. 7.

20 See, for example, Leslie Dewart, *The Future of Belief* (New York: Herder & Herder, 1965), and Gregory Baum, ed., *The Future of Belief Debate* (New York: Herder & Herder, 1967).

21 Jürgen Moltmann, *Hope and Planning* (New York: Harper & Row, 1971), p. 116.

22 Fred Polak, *Prognostics* (Amsterdam: Elsevier Company, 1971), p. 45.

23 Amos Wilder, *Eschatology and Ethics in the Teaching of Jesus* (New York: Harper & Row, 1954), p. 32.

24 W. D. Davies and D. Daube, *The Background of the New Testament and Its Eschatology* (Cambridge: Cambridge University Press, 1956), p. 34.

25 Bertrand Russell, *Religion and Science* (London: Oxford University Press, 1960), p. 81.

26 Jürgen Moltmann, *Hope and Planning* (New York: Harper & Row, 1971), p. 195.

27 H. H. Rowley, *The Relevance of Apocalyptic* (London: Lutterworth Press, 1963), p. 181.

28 Moltmann, *Hope and Planning*, p. 196.

29 Ibid., p. 197.

30 Rowley, *The Relevance of Apocalyptic*, p. 182.

31 D. S. Russell, *The Method and Message of Jewish Apocalyptic* (London: SCM Press, 1964), p. 140.

32 Paul Ramsey, *Fabricated Man: The Ethics of Genetic Control* (New Haven: Yale University Press, 1971), p. 27.

33 Leon R. Kass, "The New Biology: What Price Relieving Man's Estate?" *Science* (November 19, 1972), pp. 770-88.

34 Schubert Ogden, *The Reality of God and Other Essays* (London: SCM Press, 1967), p. 157.

Chapter 4. The Pursuit of Happiness and the Vision of Health

1 Quoted in *Time*, special Bicentennial Issue on "The Presidents," October 1976 (Portrait of Jefferson), p. 3.

2 William McNiell, *Plagues and Peoples* (New York: Anchor, 1976).

3 Quoted in Henry Steele Commager, *Jefferson, Nationalism, and the Enlightenment* (New York: Braziller, 1975).

4 John Adams, quoted in Commager, p. 18.

5 Thomas Jefferson, quoted in Commager, p. 19.

6 Commager, p. 25.

7 Dag Hammarskjöld, *Markings* (New York: Alfred A. Knopf, 1964), p. xvi.

8 John F. Kennedy, quoted in Robert Bellah, "Civil Religion in America" (New York: American Academy of Arts and Sciences), *Daedalus*, Winter 1967, p. 37.

9 William Osler, *The Old Humanities and the New Sciences* (New York: Houghton-Mifflin Co., 1920), pp. 2ff.

10 Michael De Bakey, "The Medical Prognosis: Favorable, Treatable, Curable," *Saturday Review World*, August 24, 1974, p. 46.

11 *U.S. News and World Report*, March 3, 1975, p. 42.

12 Thomas Jefferson, quoted in Henry Wilder Foote, *The Religion of Thomas Jefferson* (Boston: Beacon Press, 1947), p. 4.

13 Ibid., p. 5.

14 Hans Selye, *The Stress of Life* (New York: McGraw Hill, 1950), p. 274.

15 G. B. Shaw, "Preface to the Doctor's Dilemma," in *Prefaces by Bernard Shaw* (London: Constable, 1934), p. 280.

16 See the special issue of *Psychology Today* (August 1975) on "the pursuit of happiness."

17 See Commager, *Jefferson, Nationalism, and the Enlightenment*, p. 108.

18 See Paul Starr, "The Politics of Therapeutic Nihilism" in *The Hastings Center Report*, Oct. 1976, pp. 24ff.

19 Hubert Humphrey, "Our Surplus Citizens: How America Wastes Its Human Resources," *Saturday Review* (August 7, 1976), p. 7.

20 Ivan Illich, *Medical Nemesis* (New York: Pantheon, 1976), p. 6.

21 See Kenneth Vaux, "Religion and Health," *Preventive Medicine*, Dec. 1976.

22 Hans Jonas, "The Burden and Blessing of Mortality," *Hastings Center Report*, Jan./Feb. 1992, pp. 34ff.

23 Thomas Jefferson, *The Writings of Thomas Jefferson, Vol. 15*, ed. Lipscomb and Bergh (Washington D.C., 1903), pp. 95-97.

24 Pierre Teilhard de Chardin, from *Le Milieu Divin*, in *Suffering* (New York: Harper & Row, 1975), pp. 57-58.

25 *Pittsburgh Press*, May 17, 1964.

26 Quoted in Commager, *Jefferson, Nationalism, and the Enlightenment*, p. 108.

Chapter 5. Case Studies

1 *American Medical News*, October 9, 1981. P.N. I counseled the family and consulted with Roman Catholic Ethicist Richard McCormick, finding their decision not to feed and let die normally acceptable. A dozen years later, one son had died after four years of intense suffering in an intensive-care setting. The stronger brother has survived and is doing quite well. The family has split. Ethical decisions always occur in an atmosphere of doubt and risk, guilt, shame, hope, and forgiveness.

2 William Stringfellow, *An Ethic for Christians and Other Aliens in a Strange Land* (Waco, Tex.: Word, 1973), p. 77.

3 "Which twin is to live?: Defects of fetus treated before birth," *The Chicago Catholic*, October 30, 1987, p. 1. See also *Chicago Tribune*, November 5, 1981, pp. 1, 12.

4 *Chicago Tribune*, November 10, 1981.
5 Immanuel Jakobovits, "Judaism," *The Encyclopedia of Bioethics* (New York: Macmillan Free Press, 1978), p. 794.
6 Quoted in Charles Webster, *The Great Instauration* (New York: Holmes & Meier, 1975), p. 8.
7 Blackstone, *Commentaries on the Law of England, Book 4*, chap. 14, p. 23.
8 George B. Shaw, *Doctor's Dilemma* (New York: Penguin, 1937), p. 270.
9 Thomas Hardy, *Jude the Obscure* (New York: Bantam, 1895), p. 406.
10 Nietzsche, *Joyful Wisdom: The Philosophy of Nietzsche* (New York: Mentor Press, 1965), p. 640.